SUNDAY RISING

POEMS BY PATRICIA CLARK

MICHIGAN STATE UNIVERSITY PRESS ▪ *East Lansing*

⊚ The paper used in this publication meets the minimum requirements
of ANSI/NISO Z39.48-1992 (R 1997) (Permanence of Paper).

 Michigan State University Press
East Lansing, Michigan 48823-5245

Printed and bound in the United States of America.

19 18 17 16 15 14 13   1 2 3 4 5 6 7 8 9 10

LIBRARY OF CONGRESS CATALOGING-IN-PUBLICATION DATA
Clark, Patricia, 1951–
Sunday rising : poems / by Patricia Clark.
p. cm.
ISBN 978-1-60917-354-8 (ebook) / ISBN 978-1-61186-068-9 (pbk. : alk. paper)
I. Title.
PS3553.L2876S86 2013
811'.54—dc23
2012028149

Book design by Charlie Sharp, Sharp Des!gns, Lansing, Michigan
Cover design by Erin Kirk New.
Cover art is *Ascension* © 2012 by Stan Krohmer and is used courtesy of the artist.

g green
press
INITIATIVE Michigan State University Press is a member of the Green Press
Initiative and is committed to developing and encouraging
ecologically responsible publishing practices. For more information about
the Green Press Initiative and the use of recycled paper in book publishing,
please visit *www.greenpressinitiative.org.*

Visit Michigan State University Press on the World Wide Web at
www.msupress.org

SUNDAY RISING

for my sisters,
Ann, Kathy, Jean, and Chris,
who have led the way

A soul tears itself from the body and soars.

—Czeslaw Milosz, "Second Space"

Contents

I.

Risen from the Underworld

Arranged on slabs of sedimentary rock, rough-edged,
            beige-gray with umber streaks,
     circle of three figures sitting upright, holding knees in postures of
            deep concentration as though facing
each other over a glittering pool or a campfire,
     finding contemplation in its flames.

Gray silvered stainless steel letters form their
            human husks—heads, necks and backs, shoulders, arms.

    I imagine them risen up, like smoke, from the underworld,
journeying here to pause, immobile, as though to instruct us in some
            kindred wisdom—

like knights whose questing days have gone, heavy chain-
            mail armor exchanged for lighter stuff worn now as skin.
                 Not minding, they hunch without faces, mouths or eyes,
     one indistinguishable from the other two.

Perhaps they form a group of three muses—
            quirky figures come to applaud efforts at speech,
     raw tries at understanding, while clouds go whiffing through the
            alphabet.

        Stay seated here for eons in a green meadow,
     trusting your own sweet time, they offer up,
            until thoughts and sentences swirl together from
verbs, nouns, articles, particles.

Whoever they might be, uptilted on floes of Spanish stone,
     xeno-shapes posing quietly together, do they seem to

yearn toward each other? Voices of those gone are drifting, zigzagging through, a rough music laced with cicadas, grackles, flies.

Autumn on the Seine, Argenteuil

Two banks, one golden, one green,
        and in the center, the town
      ahead, with a spire needling up,
   a puncture into clouds,
        and vague suggestions
of industry—buildings, smoke, and noise.

What I love along the bank are the skiffs
        drawn up, five or more
      at the golden side, the first boat
   a bright russet like a horizontal flame
        on water,
the next two mauve, one a sailboat,
        one not.

The ochre-gold spills down from the cottonwoods,
        pouring under the hulls,
      entering the river with the same
   intensity of burning
        we see in life at its peak,
or life with the flame
      threatening to go out.

In a month the trees will be masts
        bare as the boats,
    the man we know, ill with a fatal brain tumor,
  will be gone—the Grand River
        burnished with ochre and red
    as the Seine is,
cooling air hinting at winter's knives.

One bank green in the painting,
       green going away,
    and the river placid, calm—
      in the center of it—
  the flowing never ceasing, rhythm of moon,
sun, the turning earth, pulling it outward,
        eternal, restless, to the maw of the sea.

Oscine

Singing tribes, from hidden perches, from stems
  and blossoms—honeysuckle, trumpet vine,
  clematis—from a cottonwood's high branch
or the top spire of the white pine,
  this warbling, crooning, cooing.

Seldom from the ground, from a low place—why
  is that? Some fasthold with security,
  safety, a haven—or something about shade, semi-
dark, coolness, looking out
  and then to lift one's voice, here.

From the ecotone, edges, margins, trees into field,
  lawn into hem of the woods,
  riverine bank, creek, tree limb,
from the tree's dark trunk, rain-slick,
  from the leaf's umbrella-shade.

Song to braid this new day or darkening gloom,
  notes to send out, testing what the voice
  can do—trills, legato, runs and rasps,
rattle of tongue against palate, mix of ecstasy,
  elegy, sound into art.

Tomorrow Marks Six Years

A stone for breakfast.
Wintry walk with the dog
who bounces no matter what.

Later some few hours,
book in hand, lamplight pooled.
She's on my mind tonight, still.

Scrabbling for a piece
of her—five daughters grabbed
and clawed. I've got her bad foot.

Someone's caught her hands,
one sister held her heart.
I'm trying to admire

bunion, hammer toe.
A gift from her to me—
to take, treasure, and to hold.

Slippers, bedtime moves.
My right foot matches hers.
Mother bear leaves tracks in snow.

Aeromancy

Sundog, torrential rain,
ring around the midnight moon

Columnar light, once in minus
temps, flurries of snow:
headlights of cars shone odd,
straight up

Moisture that creeps into pages,
photographs, bones of ancestors
at Ellsworth Cottage,
Gull Lake

From these I predict—we, too,
will pass away,
perhaps without remembrance—
consider the example

Zora Perkey here, writing her name
on a book's flyleaf—
putting a line near a word
in the margin

This leaf pressed in—clover?
Here to mark a kiss?

Remember your own first—
then turn, let's smooch, and take
ourselves to the pillow-soft bed
to float, frolic

like unpredicting clouds

Winter Nests

Study their look aloft, leaf piles, stick and twig
laid down as lattice for a base, then stem upon stem
of leaves fastened and layered in together, not glue,
staple, or tape but interlock of twig and leaves,
edge and notch, heaped at a stout limb snag, some
cracked, molded, bent, some interlain with fluff,
down of breast feather or blossom, frayed catkins a bird
tugged inch by inch from the yard waste heaped
out back behind the shed where a pile mounds up,
useful to robin, crow, or red-tailed hawk, not spring
dwellings for hatching eggs, warming them, raising
a clutch but dark splotches, large, in a blasted
bare oak for a storm shield, a blizzard house when
it's this arctic, frigid—half dead landscape seared below.

Energy Economics

"We balance on a ray of light and an oxygen molecule."
—Bernd Heinrich

I want to wake up beyond the lowering sky—
    it muddies my heart, clouding who I am,
I want to extrapolate, extend and exclaim—
    this is a day, this may be the richest
    Friday of my life,
I want meals al fresco, wine aerated and silky,
I want the blowdowns in the woods to stand back up,
    rise on their roots and walk,
If I want that orange again, black and orange flashing,
    is that to want oriole or to hope for cardinal,
    not to mention tanager?
I want the great blue heron to let me linger nearby,
    allowing me to lie down under its wingspan—
When I want sunspecks, the sky stays milky, if I want cloudy,
    it drifts to stark blue clear—
I want the dream undreamed, the one where my sister turns,
    slipping her arm through his, and never comes back,
    her complaints true and loud, but forgetting
    admixtures of love—
I want building up, motives unmixed and straight
    as tree trunks can ever be—
I want flights cross-country, my West brought home again,
    I want more and yet more of it—mapwise, riverwise, Puget Sound—
I want salt and the water-licked shore, driftwood,
    mountain slope heartbreaking, rugged,
    sure, unbending stone.

Plane of Last Scattering

The image repeats, back and back in threaded time
like a hall of mirrors, a spinal column ascending,
regular, unbending, proud standard of cartilage, bone,
disc to lead us up and up. Then a flood of wheaten

gold pouring in, a groundwater carrying saffron, a hint
of crimson, palest daffodil cup blonde and waving
in sun. These might be the notches enabling us to climb
out of ourselves—and so, hand over hand, the path.

Tracery of bird flight, not mallard or heron straight
but with the woodpeckers' evading, curvy, up, down, up,
though still direct from point A to B. Abundant sheer

pleasure of repetition, the day come again—old friend—
to serve us. If learning how to live were simple flight—
or the magical extension of wings curving to cup air.

Ravine Goddess, August

She crooned, low, above the fetid smell
left by skunk overnight, then the notes
smoothed out, creamy, any ragged edges
disappearing, dissolved by rhythm, sound,
creek riffles moving downstream—though hurt
could still be heard, angling in the way a bur
catches by one prong, hanging on to fabric of shirt
or jeans—not easy to pry off, you'll try to shake
it without any luck. In the dog's hair, it works up
to a snarl, rat's nest, tangle you will have to
cut out with scissors. And always the most tender
of places—notch behind the ear, foreleg, rump
or belly hair close to the animal's sex. So try
the muzzle method—nip it out, lave with a wet tongue.

Quebrada

If the ground is torn, pebbled, cracked, showing a breakup
of ground has occurred, one leading to a rupture of landscape,
horizons, passes, this is *quebrada*. Do you hear
the lament crackling through its syllables? Oh my lost
footing, my sister, see how fissure-like all my ravines
have become. Where a mountain stream might break out
of a canyon or gully, *quebrada* the land at its source.
At one family's beginnings, five girls and only far later,
the twin boys, a last boy, the breaks. Then years of splitting,
separating, the centrifugal whirling away to a state
of entropy or call it heat death—though for a time,
no one saw the country beyond. The ground goes on quaking,
trembling, as though giants trod here. Our parents down,
deadfall trunks prone along the creek, stripped gray, bare.

Anti-Love Poem

Sometimes you want to love the person across
the room, the one glancing up from his book
with a faraway gaze, saying "if I hadn't met X,
if he hadn't written a letter for me, then you
and I wouldn't be here." Part of me refuses
to bite, won't hitch myself to his sweet misty-eyed
mood. Someone today needs to haul up a box
from the basement, start lifting each ornament
off the Christmas tree. Before the holiday,
he lay ill with a cold—if I hadn't decorated the tree
we wouldn't have to remove fragile balls or lights.
If he weren't sitting across the room, I wouldn't
need to soften my heart, look up to find his glance.
I could live in a fortress, behind stout walls.
How else to be human? How else to be saved?

My Mother's Feline Companion

It filtered back to me, her habit of TVs left on
blaring in empty rooms, one upstairs, one down—

talk radio, too, droning in the bedroom or bath, I think
it showed how far she had traveled in this world

to possess so many appliances, speaking ones,
at that—and what if you suddenly had to pee,

not wanting to miss what the pet therapist
advised about talking to your dog or cat,

telling them right out, plain, "I'll be gone
three days but Joey will come in to feed you."

My mother collapsed, that electrical slump,
because her cat died a few days before, let's admit it,

the one named Boy George because of errors made,
early on, with gender identification. White furred thing,

scrawny, sunken in, the two were compatriots to the end.
I want to go back, these many years later,

to the lobby where my mother fell on her face—
prow of her nose hitting first. No way to go.

I cushion her fall, angel of that Tacoma morning,
laying her down somewhere sweetly cushiony

with the cat—last breaths taken on the air together.

Wreath for the Red Admiral

A ragged morning with a tattered wing
like the red admiral yesterday's breeze
    carried into the back garden

up from the ravine, up from a sheltered spot
it had found in sunlight where it was contemplating
    warmth by basking in it.

The season two weeks ahead of itself, farmers
worried about the cherry crop—in orchards, they speak
    like painters, "pink too early."

How we waited all winter for sun, warmth,
to return, as hungry for it as we were for meat,
    for bread, for each other—

common here, not migrating as far as the monarch,
the red admiral emerges any time of year—
    from a tree-high burrow hole, borrowed,

or from an inch-thick space under cottonwood bark.
Admire its black wings edged with red-orange bands—
    white scallops on the tips.

I want to learn, living, how to be ragged on the wing
before another, loving the sun in each fiber and cell, not
    hiding where it's torn.

After Franz Marc's *The Red Deer* (1912)

The apocalyptic future the artist saw long ago
shudders behind headlines in summer 2010—

red deer, necks snaking up to heads
sculpted finely, black noses and coal dark eyes—

white throats, bellies blushed with a smudge
bluish gray, otherwise downy and pale.

And the river's bloodied where they stand—
what will they drink? They cannot sip fiery

rouged water, wading there, eating the palms
or Solomon's seal bending along the bank—

I grow frightened by the pale looming ghosts,
eyeless, icy cold, in the background—

my nightmare lurks there, dead, denuded world
that we created with our waste, our greed.

Elegy for Wilma

Along the river in November, thin red canes bend,
bramble of some berry I can't identify.

Dark brown pods, half a finger's length,
burst open to show white filaments,

each carrying a nugget at its tip, frail cargo,
half of them gone on the wind.

I notice how each plant finishes the year,
milkweed, motherwort, everlasting pea.

My friend gone on a journey south, down through
Ohio fields, to comfort her twin sister must sit,

by now, at her deathbed, touching warm skin
of a hand that matches her own, both half

of a split egg some seventy years ago—
as the room fills with music, light,

then grays, thickening, only to drain of dark,
come dawn, then starting the cycle again.

Can the native plants along the river, grasses too,
daylilies, tell us anything of foreboding?

When the northeast wind blows, skidding across water,
they bend, and papery capsules crack, quite

predictably, along the seams, rattled seeds
spilling to earth, not knowing the harder part

of winter's coming. They ready for it as they can,
with dispersal, needing no word for it.

II.

Until It Speaks

Maybe my ears are made
mostly for reasons of symmetry,
balance like the way I feel
about rivers. You can't really
get them to speak to you
with a short acquaintance.
If you walk there on a first
or second try, notice
frogs taking leave of the bank
exclaiming something in frog
language, maybe "eek!"
And you check out a blue
rowboat pensive as a
lover moored and forlorn
at a landing. Walked half
a mile, nothing yet
spilled into the ears, wrought
into words. For starters,
you have to be willing to step
into the long grasses, beyond,
to pass the soothsayer's
maison, recently abandoned
upon her death, to go there
again at dawn, then after dark
to the Garonne's banks. What did
you say you were willing
to do? Think a year
or more. Think learning
a new palette of riverine
words. There is one
dictionary for its dialect,
left open at the soothsayer's

desk, a pencil mark
in the margin at the word
raiment. Isn't it how
we dress our indifference?
As though anyone were coming
strolling along to be fooled.

Rocks and Minerals

I stood as sure of him
as stone, as gravity, as
white oak tree trunk eighty feet
up in the yard, *solid*,
I called him when others
named him air, cloud, pine
needle cluster fragile, wisp
of seed blown from a milkweed,
flower of chocolate joe-pye
weed, dandelion. Should
never have slept sure of him
as sun touching forearm skin
after winter's length, as pillow
for my sore head. Others
warned but I thought no,
not him, not me, this
substance is feldspar,
epidote, limestone,
even better—dolomite.
Instead, pussy willow, snow-
melt, sandstone worn by
water, he cannot stay
true to season, lover,
friend. The gypsum mine
I climbed down into, late
summer, gaped wide halls
in some parts, others
narrow passageways where
we had to stoop, slog through water
and muck before coming
out, a few of us still bent over—
I had worn the wrong boots,

smooth soles with no tread—
and, thank the moon, a few
others held me up, I would
have gone down flat.

Tent Caterpillars

Terrible to look at them closely
through gauzy webbing,
how they writhe and twist,
a jumbled mass, squirming,
faceless, mouthparts moving, chewing—
are they eating the excretions
from others in their nest?

Sometimes men seize on a gem,
an idea of burning them out
with a gas-soaked rag held aloft
like a torch on a long pole—
the whoosh as the rag lights, an awful
purse-shaped bag of flame
blackening as the insects
ignite, consumed.

Kill the infestation but not
to light the shed—its wood
so crackling dry it wouldn't take
much, the sun's rays concentrated
on a nailhead heating up, spontaneously
combusting the nearby slats,
crumbling brown boards.

And the woods themselves, not to
stumble, toe caught on Virginia creeper,
ankle turned on a leaf pile or log,
not to drop the pole, or let this
caterpillar nest-fire drop straight down,

liquid melt setting duff, mounded oak leaves,
deadfalls, last year's Christmas tree ablaze—

and if you do—the quickness with which
it catches, runs, blows up to the treetops—
lighting them. How many nightmares
of fiery extinction, this purge to destroy
a spreading pest but rescue the cottonwood?
How many visions of a thing burned clean,
the mass destroyed, what's left made
beautiful by riddance, a scouring flame?

Near Paradise, Michigan: Crushed

Whatever RV or motor home this once was
it lies crumpled now
like a piece of stiff white paper

with aqua window shutters
its roof gathering the pine's needles and cones
with each wind gust

making a soft bed
for mourning doves or a nesting wren.
What has crawled inside to snooze?

Consider the ant, the vole,
the striped chipmunk who likes company.
Virginia creeper goes twining its way

around axle, tires, CV joints,
tie rods, sway bars, bumper and latch.
Cinnamon fern now waves its fronds

against floorboards, deck, against walls
broken and bent by a storm's blowdown
branches and thick trunks.

Who were the humans driving off to explore
together in this home on wheels
spinning and humming down the highway?

When the nor'easter kicks up across the meadow
sometimes a woman's voice sails out
clear as a bird, then a man's voice braids in—

a song about a valley, ravine, meadow, creek,
celebrating a river, or a rocky shore, hands
rowing them in, hands crossing a salt-stained bow.

Air Like a Sea

I noticed the willow's long fronds
    hung down crimped
      like ringlets
    just unwrapped—
        and some birdsong,

notably the robin's, at midday
    came out ragged,
      a bit rusty
    and not so liquid—
        new leaves bore a fuzz

like the newborn's fontanel,
    without the throb,
      though everything
on the wing seemed to be alighting,
      building, catching up

a catkin in its beak or scouting
    for worms or grubs.
      I wanted to place a finger
on the day's pulse,
      making it pause—

my fingernails like shells,
    the day's air a sea rolling in,
      filling space around me,
    raising the beached kelp
        to sway alive, like hair.

Near Paradise, Michigan: Brown Cabin, Roof with a Green Stripe

Whoever lived here once, female or male, face recognizable or not,
packed up in a hurry, snatching from drawers and hooks a shirt, a hat,
cramming earrings into pockets, balled socks into shoes,
pitching a few books into a canvas bag, crossing the sill,
closing the door, forgetting the lock.

Walking away through oat-eared grass from this cabin
by a burned-out tree, whoever left made a lingering survey
of the front door, regretting the rusty stain smeared
down the white frame, the missing screen and knob,
intending to return with hammer, spackle, and paint.

Whoever slept here once, a single bed, white percale sheets,
piled her head by the window, drafty or not,
slept entranced by the peepers' chorus from the creek, the song
of the great northern owl on the wing and the hunt,
stoked the fire before sleeping, woke to it cold.

Dreaming here once, ditching sleep one summer night
for the stars, someone lay out prone on the ground with a man
counting, ticking off, adding up moments, meteors, more,
moving on to cats, loved objects, an enamelware pitcher or two,
books neat on shelves or heaped on a chair, till sleep came.

Whoever moved, in love, out of this place vowed to return,
crafting a path by stacking cairns of stones, trees marked higher
than snowbank with a blaze, twigs snapped in half and balanced
on a branch, a blue jay's feather wedged in a notch,
obedient plant picked, petal by purple, a drifted winding trail.

Rockweed, Knotted Wrack, Dead Man's Fingers

This is the rocky intertidal—stones,
  boulders, slabs tumbled together,
 thrown up here, left jagged by storms
    that batter land,
   and these the plants and algae
 wedged into crevices, cracks, sheer rockface.

Three levels of tide pools like stepping into caves,
  caverns of the mind as you go down—
 our guide warns that dark means
    most slippery—take care and crouch
   low to the ground, make a handhold
 of seaweed, surprisingly strong
    where it adheres.

Now sea anemone, amphipods, tortoiseshell limpets—
  tough attachers, limpets make their move
 at high tide, after, moving over rock
    to clean off, take in,
 what algae has stuck to stone, a banquet
   with a tang of sea salt, Atlantic air.

Discarded at the high tide line before descent—
  baggage of notebook, pen, field guide,
 lotions and spray to ward off bugs,
    the sun. Why so often
   at the shore, seaside, the margin, the brief
 deep, intimate talk? I barely know
    these people of half a day.

Carl mentions, first, the friends they partied with
  of a summer night, how two days later,

after the stroke, the woman lay blind,
        without speech or movement—
Beth, leaning close to him, laughs
        at her own mortality, says prednisone, shunt.

Turning over a rock or two, a hand thrust in
        to the wrist—dog whelk, red-nose clam,
hermit crab lugging its spiral shell-home
        and green crab, rock crab,
barnacle. The tide pool tales are ones
        of adapting, small and large changes—
        some sudden, slow, fixed—

to adverse circumstances—the weather, tides,
        temperature going up or down, variation in food
source or amount. Knotted wrack over time evolving
        float bladders from its own membrane
to keep foliage lifted up—seeking life-
        giving light.

Of this hour only, we find ease against coastal boulders,
        themselves soaking up sun.
Why go back now, step inside?
        No other life than this—
the raw sea air, pungent pools of scrabbling life
        and death—everywhere you look scraps of claw,
        exoskeleton, bleached, abandoned.

Viewshed

A twenty-inch feather with black bars. Stones I've picked up.
An acorn with its cap beside it like a cup.

Chunks of gypsum from a mine I explored,
a postcard of a heron—eye glittering, not bored.

Pens and pencils nestled in a metal box.
A magnifying glass for peering at flowers and rocks.

A clump of lichen, gray blue, smelling like smoke.
One pressed leaf with a black spot—from an eighty-foot oak.

Dusty gold wing of a half-eaten moth—
so slender it wriggled in, hid under a cloth.

A three-pronged branch tip—with unopened buds.
Whatever ripe swelling, they ended up duds.

Ahead through the glass stand our woods going bare—
pine needles, dappled ground, color smearing the air.

Poem Ending with a Line from Tranströmer

First a drumming—fast, pulse, with urgent beats.
A running, rushing off at roof-edge, down—
then the tempo slowing, scattered beats, soft.

Birdsong from American robins, our
elegists. Not dusk, this leaf-dusk shimmers,
shines with rain-smeared light, sky opalescent.

Slanted tin roof reverberates with each
struck drop—musical threnody of day.
Beautiful slag of experiences.

Late Letter to Hugo

I invoked your name, dear man,
yesterday in Kalamazoo, Michigan—
to a group of art teachers who did not know

how to love you yet. They wanted to,
I assure you. They came in a range
of ages, colors, shapes.

Our focus was poems and how to
nurture them, seedlings with various
fruit to come, though in my mind I saw

heirloom tomatoes, Boxcar Willie, Black Krim,
and Peach. I think you would like
these tomatoes, Dick, just beginning

to ripen in early August heat. Ditto
the teachers. The only male, a small
fellow named Fred, wrote a poem inspired by a boy

with a hat on his head, two cats teetering
on top. The black and white photo showed the kid
with a half smile, eyes hidden

by the brim, maybe an Irish lad with a past
as checkered as his hat. All over
the world, boys grow up with cats,

brimmed caps, in cities and towns needing
to find joy. Sometimes it can be teased out,
even from shadow. Signing off, pal, with love.

Helleborus Orientalis

Sometimes I notice snow lying blue
or silvery green under trees, close to water,
and rarely ever a time
of thaw when snow is gone, revealing flowers—
except for my backyard Lenten rose, a creation of pure adagio,
leaves below a blossom drooping down.

I wanted to go down
near water just to see if I could call it blue,
instead it gleamed silver, or gray green like an adagio
both dreamy and sorrowful. Can water
make a kind of music? The current moves in waves, flowers
over the dam past all the fishermen marking time

with fly rods and beautiful line flexing out like time,
snaking along in air until it lies down,
drifting, on water. The figures bloom like tall flowers
out in mid-river where the water moves blue
but rapid. Imagine the force of water—
they brace against it, step and hold like an adagio

movement between *allegro* and *allegro assai*. The adagio
often marks the most tender moments, when time
in Mozart's 23rd piano concerto slows, watery
piano notes calling in the orchestra. When the baton comes down
at the end, listeners have been riding a blue
wave of feeling and thought. What idea, then, couldn't flower

and become not just an ordinary flower—
but the pale blush of a Lenten rose? It's the adagio
period between winter's closed face and the thaw's blue
sky. Let's call it rebirth: watching time,

light lengthening over a span of days with catkins downy
and red dangling from the trees. Isn't that water

dripping from a green metal roof? What watery
selves we all are! The desire to be rooted in place, to flower
as we must, sending one's roots down, and down.
This opposes the fragile blossom's life, adagio
pure and simple. Here is full expression in time
marked by beauty and music, brief and blue.

I swear I saw the color of snow, of water and time—
not in a shade of blue but flowering in pure repose.
Fading adagio, a Lenten rose before its day came down.

Wood Not Yet Out

Shift in light that signals what we've
come through—and still the tree skeletons,
oak and hardwood, the scattered crisp
tatters of a few leaves. Tracks in snow
soften more each day—whatever passed here
left a few belly hairs, tail bristles caught
on the brush pile's edge. I step on down,
through, feeling my weight snap something hidden
underfoot, then a vine tangles my boot.
Water's my only destination, seeing it move,
sinking in at the muddy lip where whitetails
stand, brown lookout statues before they cross.
Where water carves under bank and roots,
dark hollows show where winter's fears have lain.

Kingston Plains

White has robbed us of the horizon
    darkening the evergreens
and the stand of tall ones is like a mind

refusing to yield, holding its beliefs, saying no
    in unison—
through trunk, tip and feathered branch—

see its shape cast down
    into the shallow wetland pool
fragrant with arrowroot, cattail, sedge—

acidic soil flourishing the wild blueberries
    pea-sized and dusky
ripening in late summer for plundering

in mouthfuls by the black bear
    roaming solo on this plain.
Dream landscape of the heart,

stand of evergreens sailing
    under the corn moon before
snow flies, piling in extravagant furls and cliffs.

By Clear and Clear: Riverside, Midday

The old self dying away, you can feel it, can hear
a skeletal crack, then snap, as a ridgeline
breaks all down the thorax, the bony carapace
splitting, a faint odor lifting off, burnt hair
and a wet sizzle, the new lying there almost fetid
with freshness, with its own moist softness—
fetal, or maybe just larval, tender, exposed.
On all sides water, this again, the spit of land
liminal, pelagic, far from dry, your very steps
leaving an imprint in grass. Tomorrow you could return,
matching your prints to the day before—this day—
a child's game. Is that where the fractures go?
Now you walk emancipated, on the loose—out of the house,
its stale air, parents gone at last—grown-up, free.

After Hiroshige

Two men working in skiffs
        on the River Serba—
           one poling a full load of wood bundled
for fires on shore
        and another reaching in with a gaff,
     wrist wet, lapped by water, to check
the river's depth, his rice plants—
        are the seed heads full?
Is the crop ready for harvesting?

A full moon balloons half a tree height
        above the horizon—
        both men too busy to notice
how it is snagged
        in the branches of a willow swept
     nearly bare, willow leaning
identically as the second man bends,
        shore reeds tipped to the right
also, marked by prevailing wind.

Good to focus on the task
        at hand, afloat on river water—
        if you look up at sky, the star field
as I did one recent morning—
        in mid-footfall on blacktop
     down a darkened street with the dog,
counting by tens up to one hundred,
        two hundred before
slowing, letting breath huff out—.

If one pauses to look, staring,
        the brittle icy stars can

shock you—what else besides
the heavens neglected
      by me for months?
   Now a slap of recognition,
this sliding back into my skin—
            diamond-white stars, black sky,
the hunter's figure showing clearly.

I embraced every contradiction of newfound
            sight, the vast distance from the River Serba
      to this place, the utter loveliness of being
a speck on a watery planet wobbling through space.
      The two men go on bending to their task,
   I step outside in dark with the dog—
and wood heaped on that distant shore
            crackles a fragrant fire, red-gold flame
gleaming by wet rocks, one where I warm my hands.

Heron, in Sunlight

It glittered, bent its neck,
　　　rummaged in its breast feathers
　　for a speck of dirt, a flea,

and along I came with the dog,
　　　walking, watching as we do—
　　most ordinary of all mornings—

That's it, my dear. No sweet
　　　promise of rescue, transport
　　out of time—let's say

we were stuck in time, pinned—
　　　triad of self, dog, bird—
　　before the moment went whirling

away, a flock of goldfinches
　　　wrinkled by, all scatter, burble,
　　unstraight line, snippet of song.

Burial Underwear

Saying the words *My father died*
for the first time, I felt my face
crumple like a creek bed undermined
by rushing water, the giving way
almost causing a sob to escape
in front of strangers at the airport
ticket counter where gray carpet
matched January skies. I wanted
to reach Seattle to hold him one
last time but had missed, by twelve hours,
my chance. Later, the funeral director's face
contorted when I asked could I see his body
before the embalming, the makeup
and clothes. *You don't want to see him*
like that, she said. Mother and I stood
together at the closet of his beautiful suits—
not expensive cashmere jackets but frayed
corduroy, elbows and cuffs, neat slacks, none
recently worn but still fragrant
with his skin, underarms, hair.
Together we picked out a pale yellow
dress shirt, jacket and pants the rich
brown of his hair long ago, forgetting socks,
underwear. Leaning over the casket
to kiss him goodbye, I felt the chilly
metal box pillowed inside with silk—
thinking how he lay so distinguished
there either with no underwear
or wearing some other man's garment
into the grave. My father once wore
handsome boxers, paisley, a small print—

tan, an olive green, and as a young girl I would
fold them, pet them almost, dreaming of days
ahead when I would know all the great
and profound mysteries.

III.

Olentangy Elegy

1.

Variant names
for the Olentangy River

stone for your knife stream

olentangy
whetstone creek
whetstone river
whitestone creek

2.

Down from Michigan
pass the mosque gleaming white
and gold
in northern Ohio

cross over the Mad River
no variant names

pass by cornfield
cornfield

Do not think Italy
but bean
when you say Lima

3.

Delaware State Park Reservoir built
the year I was born

Did any of us care

about Ohio then?

Washington State beaches rocking us,
tidal, with seawater—

And when did your sister arrive?

4.
We cut up onions, green
pepper,
made do with tomatoes
canned, Marzano ones from volcanic
soil of Italy—
crushed them

took out bags
of frozen corn kernels
blanched, cut off
cobs in late summer
now plump still

Even in winter the thick
corn-veggie soup fragrant

when we walked back from
Mulick Park, sledding

orange disk sliding
matching the full moon
dog's tail tipped white
waving

goodbye,
last good memory

5.
The Olentangy provides
drinking water for Delaware County

mouth dry these many
months, lips dry, parched

unable to take a sip

6.
Shale to make your knife
sharp

all the better to cut
you with, my dear

names mistaken
olentangy really means

river of the red face paint

7.
What does marriage mean
if not a new
cleaving?

Does she cleave to him?

Maybe you are jealous,

maybe the bars on the windows,
the double locked doors,
maybe the twin dogs
named, adored, make you
jealous?

I only desire
her happiness.

8.
Tensions

The pull in different
directions

early learned competition
hard to trust others

brother and sister love
sister to sister love
mother love
husband love

when our parents die
ground shifts underfoot

9.
Down into Ohio, early October

Wapakoneta
when light leaves the fields
dark green, green

then a space between the rows
of corn where a person could

slip in and disappear

   10.
My sister became a Buddhist
kneeling on the black pillow
in postures of meditation

incense
a holy shrine
visits to hear
the Dalai Lama speak

Did I really make jokes about her
not wanting to kill anything?

Staying over, alone, those many years ago
at her Seattle apartment
fleas feasted all night long
on my ankles, wrists

I bought a can of Raid,
spraying it in bursts
of cloud

I slept secure that night
in my own reasoning

Was I annihilating my sister?
I sprayed the poison

and slept without dreaming

11.

Whitestone creek
Olentangy sharpening knives

And the only white stones
for miles around are graves

Shining white in August's dark
with crosses, symbols, etched names

gathering rainwater, moss

12.

That time of the fleas
was twenty years ago, in another state

and my sister Christina never knew

First marriages gone, then,
for both of us

Both finding home, the Midwest,
finding our way with new men,
no babies

far from our birth homes
far from our family

13.

How our mother would say, *watch out:*

I'm on the warpath today.

My method was to move
far away, counting the states
between us

14.
Growing up, we possessed rivers, multitudes,
among many children, lively in tents and rooms

Puyallup River near our house
fishing near Commencement Bay

The Satsop River all carefree
summer, floating

And Indian Mary, the last time
camping

I see the campground still

15.
Chris showed me the photo
after the funeral—

Father had already been gone
seven years

Mother in sunlight, eyes closed,
face lifted

Her face glowed

radiant, already heading

to another place

16.
Rivers, creeks, small
tributaries

The headwaters from which
they all come

water will find
a way,

seek a low spot

17.
*If you're finished with gallivanting
around*, Mother would say,

*If you could take off your glad
rags and get to work—*

18.
If we could live in peace
bury the hatchet

sharpen knives and then
slice bread and not each other

If the spell could send
the wicked witch into the forest

forever

19.
For eleven years I watched
one broken tree

that may or may not mark
a boundary of our land

rumor said, struck by lightning

There is not one mark
to prove it

I am noting
its disintegration

20.
Olentangy, the healing source
water brings

people picking up cans, plastic bottles,
trash, rusted oil cans

Water once again riffling,
clear and sweet

Two sisters wading in the water,
feet white as stones

shining through water

And a legend begins,
Midwestern tales of hardwood forests,
yearly renewal

And sometimes the bedrock
dolomite
chert, Chilton, flint

will not allow roots to dig down

on the Maine coast, firs grow forty or fifty feet tall,
on Orr's Island,
liable to tipping

topsoil thin, they barely hold on

Begin a new legend, if you can—

21.
When Father was dying
(only seventy-three years old),
he said *no regrets at all.*

His favorite brother Earl had died
overseas, a jeep accident during World War II

The only thing, he would say,
I wish I'd had a sister.

IV.

Sunday Rising

Like hunched women wearing red
babushkas, the wild turkeys came
stepping east through two-leaved
drooping mayapple up to their
shoulders. A weekend, they had slept
late like the rest of the neighborhood,
dapple down pillows of blossom fall,
pollen from the tall white oaks,
petals drifted from the early bloom
of our magnolia. Now the rose-
breasted grosbeak uptilts itself
on a branch to gobble a bug, then
drops off and flies. A moment ago
I turned—to find a woodchuck standing
on its hind legs staring right at me.
Together we played the childhood
game called "Statue," seeing which
of us could freeze the longest.
As the sun reached high
enough to touch my right arm
through the leaded glass window,
also flooding the nearby Miss Kim lilac
with light and warmth, it was a day
worth noting, which is to say
any day we can rise out of our-
selves. The nuns had a one-note
story they told over and again,
how the flesh, seductive, had to be
mortified, how Satan played tricks
using pleasure. If Saint Lucy had taken
advice, she would not have been forced
by sin to tear out her own eyes, nor

Saint Catherine sent rolling, burning,
on that wooden wheel—follow Saint
John, instead, and don the hair shirt
maggots could burrow under. At eight,
I tied a rough cord under my Peter Pan
blouse, bolero, and skirt, to chafe
and bind my waist, to scratch it
raw, perhaps, wearing it for days,
then, kneeling, I offered up
silent suffering for Jesus. If I tried,
now, across distances and time, to unlock
the hearts of Sisters Madeleva and Gabrielle
at Visitation School, I could not turn
the rusty key and as for that girl-who-would-
grow-to-be-me, I see the gold-brown
cord, the knot she tied weaving
ends in and out, but I cannot glimpse
her face. The untying of the knot
remains a mystery. Here the June day
comes up sweet and chill, and I do not
attend to steeple bells tolling across
Sunday air, using instead a red trowel
and my own good hands, planting yellow
daisies, upright grasses, and trailing
hopvine in these twin chapels-
of-the-window-box, near the wide open
church-of-the-fragrant-earth.

Cento

Although things vanish, are what mark our vanishing—
Homer ready to be led around the known globe—
Eight days ago I stood where he stood.
The shadows of the floating world
                              huddle beneath their objects.
How I thought of several explanations for your grief
But the wind has sown loose dreams
On one side, the soul wanders.
So cruel then that each star be our jewel
The high windows. The statues. The grand
Brothers and sisters, who live after us

Ghosts That Need Consoling

There's a black smear, low on the door-glass,
as though something tried to enter here overnight,
this place of books and a desk, my workplace.

Not a paw print exactly but an oily three-inch smudge
with particles visible—stomach contents or shit
the only two options, I think. Five panes

in the door, narrow, from top of the door
to its base, where I step in from blue schist,
a wedge-shaped slab that comes to an arrow point.

I'm the arrow, riding the red horse, tail out,
and me without saddle, bridle, reins—
arms out, too, like a warrior on the fly.

If there are bears nearby, as I believe,
maybe there's a way to learn their lore, a path
through dark woods by scent, feel, or a star.

There's an orange leaf down below on green—
glowing like a starfish on a piling in the sea.
I'm going there, no one can stop me—lost,

I'll find a bear or steer my way by dead
reckoning. Something needs settling, clearing
up, consoling—I told you something wailed

in the woods at night. It's what wants in.

Missing

Overhead, auburn light was gilded, then flat.
And the light called out to me, so I stepped outside.

Called out was a verb I could barely explain,
a subliminal tidal force into ankle-deep leaves.

Sister, will I go through another season without you?
Years ago a girl fell on a cement step

gripping a glass jar swimming with tadpoles.
They became frogs in the nearby pond,

later stunted with ulcers, extra genitals and limbs.
I hear a fatal ticking and call, again, your name.

Depressed by a Gray Mood on Tuesday, I Step Up and See a Sparrow

Eager to travel out of myself, I stand at the kitchen window,
gazing past impatiens with double fuchsia blooms,
nicotiana in Saratoga red, hopvine winding green
and faintly gold along its stems, blue trailing lobelia—
to see a chipping sparrow hopping on thin legs,
finding the one puddle on the asphalt driveway.
Then it lowers itself, dips in its
wings with white bars, splashing streaked
underparts, somehow trickling rainwater down
over its chestnut cap. It does not look my way.
If it has fears of the neighbor's gray and white cat,
or cars whizzing by on Mayfield, it doesn't show them.
Then it's gone in a flourish of droplets thrown out
boldly on June air, picking up, then trailing its trademark
chipping song from a high green branch.

If Riptides Were a Gateway

then summer's nineteen drowning victims
have been taken on their way elsewhere.

Where is it? Underwater through a slit in sand
where red flags do not flap wildly above the shore

in warning, where a woman's young sons don't sob
when their mother, gone swimming alone,

doesn't come back. August forever after means
a beach drenched in nightmare, coming darkness,

search lights, two boys waking to see her carried in.
A person's spirit may go slipping through the gateway,

breath taken there, though the earthly body's turned
back—too heavy, cartilage and bone, not ethereal enough

to make it past. She was intact, unhurt, complete
down to ankle bracelet with charms: bird, book, chair.

Nails painted, fingers and toes—which each boy longed
to kiss, faces both tear-lashed, holding hands—

before her waiting brother whispered, "It's her"—
and they put her in plastic for the morgue. Someone

must bend near, stop the action as the moon skids up
a black sky, water not allowed to have the last word,

no gateway to stars, sky, the heavens—this farewell
to a place that had felt buoyant until the wave's grip.

Zodiacal Light: A Dialogue

To see it, you look to the north
but you must not be in the north.

How can I see it then?
You must take a long drive south.

How early must I rise?
Before early light, when stars yet gleam.

Which part of the sky to study?
Learn the horizon, your planet's curve.

The description spoke of a pyramid shape—
can I expect that?

You will see dust shimmer, rise, drift.
Golden particles, astral pollen.

Could I begin driving tonight?
You will find impediments—weather, blockades.

What can I do to circumvent those?
Your way will be longer, a season's detour.

Must I give up a whole year in the wait?
Sometimes a year is the least particle.

Eyewitnesses agree: a soft glow, unearthly.
Can the last word be right? Did you listen well?

I believe in the holy name, the journey long
and good. These are not the northern lights—

they are something else, entirely.
And for this I have waited, these many years?

Near the North Sea

They are hauling a ruined boat out of the sea,
         at low tide—
             four men, two in yellow slickers,
          one barefoot—and three shaggy worn-out
                 horses, a white one
on the right head down, mane salt-soaked,
          exhausted but neck straining,
         leading the way.

Out beyond this group, five other schooners flare their sails
             on a purple sea—
          though both water and sky look boiled,
      not finished with storms—
             and the nearest ship's rigging
hangs tattered, spars and mast, a rag-shop of the heart,
          its crew limping it into shore after a night
      when wind never silenced.

The artist comes down to water as to an open place
             in the mind—
          the town abandoned behind him.
Here color, drama, and tide enchant his brush—
      now men at work picking clams, a horse and cart
silhouetted in a skim of water that mirrors the cart's
                 wooden wheels clamped by sand,
             the men's bent backs.

How can I know any shore or city of another century
             if not by art
          of the painter, photographer, the writer's pen?
      I hear the yoke of wood creaking, a man slapping
                 the horse's flank,

a boy's soft words urging her on—over splash of waves, hooves—
Come on, pull now, Dolly, Dolly—
you can do it, girl, hup, hup,
and then they're in.

It Was Raining in Middelburg

Sideways wind. Sheets of rain. A taxi, lights on.
I struggled out from the station to climb in. The Dutch
sailed by hatless, gloveless, on two wheels, cheeks ruddy.
Stan, there are bicycles everywhere, handlebar bells.
     And people do not wear helmets, reflective gear.
I will call you from the old Latin School. My bed
     there is narrow and wears a green coverlet.
There is a common room. Yogurt and eggs.
Just what you'd hope: a market square nearby
     with flowers, outside tables, umbrellas.
Love walks around, smiling. I have my own two-wheeler,
     a girl's, blue, with a lock, and saddlebags.
I am far and miss you sometimes—also eager to ride
     to Vlissingen or Veere for lunch.
Window boxes. Windows decorated with lace. And objects.
     Doors painted bright yellow or green.
A belief in the primary. Stone buildings. A canal.
And people waiting in line when the drawbridge
     rises. Right of way for bicycles.
Good spirits though not yet spring. Flowers about
     to blossom—ones growing from bulbs,
those nuggets gathering power underground:
bluebells, hyacinth, iris, narcissus, snowdrops, tulips.

Botanical Beliefs

I am letting a sweet autumn clematis stand
for everything I believe in. That is, it blooms
late, tumbling along the fence as we have bloomed,
he and I, our love childless but filled with flowers.

And sweet—think of what that hands you:
sugar, cream, butter, little mascarpone treats
with iced tops, creamy centers. Desserts puffed

and friable. Icing flavored with vanilla, swirled
onto cake. Berries, too, blushing every shade
of red from pale raspberry to the plump
Michigan blueberries we planted nearby in hope.

Last of all that, because gardeners constantly wed
themselves to hope. The clematis likes cool
feet with tendrils, leaves, buds aching toward sun.

Tell Me Again Why Western State Hospital for the Criminally Insane Should Not Frighten Me

I remember the dappled grounds below huge oaks,
bricked walkways making herringbone patterns,
our field trip group falling silent climbing down
from the bus, feeling a chill, I remember bars
on the windows, hands gripping black bars,
a far-off screaming, a shrill voice—
eyes hooded and a mouth wobbly, drooling, wet—
a bony hand, a clasp, a clutch,
a "take me home" repeated, urgently again—
I remember smells of urine, dust, skin without soap or love,
antiseptic and cement floors,
I remember an auditorium talk, an official in a suit
whose voice purred to reassure—"do not be afraid,"
but too late, too late—
and I remember trying to lift a spoon in the lunchroom,
cracking open my lips, sipping tomato soup without a slurp
but I could not swallow, could not stop staring—
feet shuffling in, ghostly forms wearing gowns,
pale shadows of people, the chosen, the marked ones,
the crazy, the sinful who must be punished, forever and ever,
amen, said the nun.

Psalm to Sing on a Frozen Morning

Brittle air but not the heart
        where it stays pumping in the chest

but I can examine shades of blue lying
on snowbank, then a fiery glittery gold, pink

Furls on the roof-edge overhang, a bulge
        ending in one dripping icicle

o light that has shifted to become generous
at evening, lingering like the chickadee

May I learn to come through as sprightly
    the bend, the bob—making a tune

may the light teach what it can
to ground, heat pulling up the stems of daffodils

o winter as teacher you have taught me
something of chill, of hook and clasp

may the searing help me note all I can
of repair, predicament, suture, scar

may I remember the browsing ones, their needs
for suet and burrow, leaf, notch—

the bend to the day ahead—
        the posture of mendicant, apostate

Where Pilgrims Pass

At night where the waters of the Garonne
and Tarn rivers come together, silky,
ducks and frogs compete, song made visible,
lines of song sent up like rich hosannahs,
like braids of smoke, where the rivers flow,
move, and in the place where a blue bridge
crosses the Garonne, it goes on
seamlessly green, sliding south
through the Pyrenees, taking the spirit
of pilgrims with it though they trudge land
instead, on a *chemin* behind a *gîte* called
River House, their boots and clothes dusty
as those travelers dozing within, dreaming
of a fifty-year flood.

River Villanelle

The river lay flat as ice, burnished shore to shore.
Smudges of color—russet, gold—shimmered across.
After months of light, someone is shutting the door.

A wake rippled like a wing, then angled, tore,
as wind picked up the waves like hems, like grass.
The river flat as liquid fire, burnished shore to shore.

Kingfisher gone, herons missing, I wanted more.
The walkers, a motley crew, are regulars who pass
after sun-crossed days when someone has closed the door.

The wake moved silver wave on wave, till four
sides made a shape which split, shattered glass.
Then the river lay flat as ice, burnished shore to shore.

The river's other side beckons some days—a chore
to reach. Could I row across? Find a buried past
after months of light, someone closing the door?

After freezing over, river ice makes a dull roar,
grinding as it tries to loosen, crack, let go with a crash.
The river lay flat as liquid fire, burning shore to shore
after months of light, then someone slamming the door.

Across Barbed Wire

Day when the clouds turn to buttermilk by 2 p.m.,
clouds churned thick and transformed to a yellowish-white,
and whatever twists you follow in country roads,
whatever meanderings take you from the main highway,
bring you to a gate, a house, a porch,
leave you at the white door in the garden, four brick walls,
    a spot to sit.

The horse noses pasture grass until you wave,
brown animal with blazed forehead crunching green
    until a hand lifts,
and the apple set out on the hand's table,
the red fruit offered on a palm,
becomes the call that beckons him,
changes into the invitation winding him
up the meadow's greening slope,
up the blazing hill.

It's mostly ridiculous how much we care,
both silly and not silly that it matters to us
who comes or sits, stays or talks,
who arrives or reclines, remains or speaks,
and yet it does—our muscles the storage places,
    hearts like attics

where dreams rise up on every side,
forests climbing inch by inch like green walls,
and hills show the scary expanses,
escarpments display all the frightening views
we thought we had left,
we hoped were gone.

No matter now.
It is not important today.
If you would not escape from me,
if you would not leave my side,
blazed horse or sweet man or kindly friend,
star-marked horse, man with eyes glittering,
    the friend who calls—

then let me say it,
then I'll pronounce it if you allow,
as the stars whirl around, a comet flares,
as galaxies wheel and a tailed ice ball goes away
    for fifteen thousand years,
how much it helps me to feed you,
exactly what it means for me to nourish you
with my own outstretched paw,
my own extended, soft-palmed hand.

Math, Architecture

I keep a basket full of riffraff stones,
a patch of bark, a length of wood,

there's a feather in inch-wide gray
white stripes, chunks of feldspar,

one piece of beach glass small enough
to be a pinkie's fingernail—in green.

I favor the organic and the mute—
they sit together well, lie at my left.

Often I count windowpanes, doing the math
of glass times glass, or door transformed

to window—two large fields so clear
the white pine steps closer with each shiver.

Slant the roof up, it'll seem larger—
from this roost I see it all, so deep

and clear your wrist will burn, if dipped
in there, air water mix and stir.

Stowaway in the Arugula

A lighter green, almost yellow,
    than the notched leaves
        of the arugula, twist-tied

in bunches with six of them
    bound together in a plastic bag.
        I glimpsed you among one,

folded like a tripod in the midst
    of that group, stems of the plant
        like bars rising to cage

you in. Dead, I thought at first, before
    seeing half of one antenna
        wave and twitch. How warm

the kitchen must have felt after
    the fridge's tomb, then a rush
        of water, draining in the sink.

Oh small traveler, grasshopper hitching
    its ride, air freight from California,
        what could I do but wish

you well. As a West Coast transplant
    myself, I wanted to say good
        luck with months of coming dark.

Let it be enough that I held you
    in my palm for a few minutes,
        carrying you outside

like an elevated host, before
setting you down (all of us go
down) into green unknown.

Exile Song

When I had no friend, I made
friends of the clover, the deer.
When I had no sunlight, I took
light banking off a wall as my warmth.

When I had no rest, I took
insomnia as a pillow, grief a pill.
When I had no dreams, I courted
the nightmares of oaks, thrashing.

When I had no sister, I rode
the ferry to Seattle calling her name.
When she blew by, I saw red
hair flashing, "Get away!"

When I sat in the temple, the stone
roared. When I sought the man's grave,
I took to the road, another coastline city.
I found it near a dumpster.

When the view of the bay was blocked,
I climbed to the rooftops—.
When I saw the island moving away,
I stood with my ankles in irons.

Where rain stops, light begins—
Open your hands, see what is cupped there.

Acknowledgments

I am grateful to the following editors and publications, including websites, where the following poems first appeared.

The Adirondack Review: "Air Like a Sea"
The Ambassador Poetry Project: "Oscine" and "Sunday Rising"
The Atlantic: "Viewshed"
Black Market Review (Liverpool, England): "By Clear and Clear: Riverside, Midday"
Cimarron Review: "Quebrada"
Controlled Burn: "Rocks and Minerals"
Driftwood: "Depressed by a Gray Mood on Tuesday, I Step Up and See a Sparrow" and "After Franz Marc's *The Red Deer*"
Escape Into Life: "Exile Song," "Ghosts That Need Consoling," "Poem Ending with a Line from Tranströmer," "Tell Me Again Why Western State Hospital for the Criminally Insane Should Not Frighten Me," "Wreath for the Red Admiral"
Imagination & Place: "Across Barbed Wire" and "Rockweed, Knotted Wrack, Dead Man's Fingers"
The Moth (Ireland): "Sunday Rising"
Northwest Review: "Burial Underwear"
Plume: "Zodiacal Light: A Dialogue"
PMS poemmemoirstory: "Winter Nests"
Praxilla: "River Villanelle" and "Tomorrow Marks Six Years"
Superstition Review: "Until It Speaks" and "Ravine Goddess, August"
Tampa Review: "Plane of Last Scattering"
Tar River Poetry: "Near Paradise, Michigan: Crushed"
Terrain.org: "Autumn on the Seine, Argenteuil" and "Tent Caterpillars"
Unsplendid: "Helleborus Orientalis"
Upstreet: "After Hiroshige"

Valparaiso Poetry Review: "Elegy for Wilma," "It Was Raining in
   Middelburg," and "Olentangy Elegy"
Wake: "If Riptides Were a Gateway"
Zócalo Public Square: "Missing"
Zone 3: "Risen from the Underworld"

Heartfelt appreciation to friends, editors, colleagues who have provided
love and support as well as critical eyes and listening ears, especially
Martha Bates and others at Michigan State University Press; Keith Tay-
lor, Michelle Boisseau, Alice Friman, Jane Hirshfield, Marilyn Kallet,
Diane Wakoski, Todd Davis, Tom Aslin, and most of all Stan Krohmer;
to those in the Writing Department and to others in the Department of
Art and Design at Grand Valley State University. Thanks to Stan, too, for
the painting on the cover. For institutional support for a sabbatical and
for travel, my thanks to Provost Gayle Davis, Dean Frederick Antczak,
and others at GVSU. And for a rainy but warm retreat when I was as-
sembling the manuscript, thanks to the Centrum Foundation in Port
Townsend, Washington.

NOTES

"Risen from the Underworld" is my response to an invitation to write about Jaume Plensa's sculpture "I, You, She, or He" at Frederik Meijer Gardens & Sculpture Park in Grand Rapids, Michigan.

"Autumn on the Seine, Argenteuil" is also the title of an 1873 Monet painting.

"Tomorrow Marks Six Years" is in memory of my mother, Norma Collins Clark (1922–2003).

"Aeromancy" references the ancient art of divination through the use of weather signs and is dedicated to Annie Ransford.

"Winter Nests" is dedicated to Jane Leonard.

"Plane of Last Scattering" owes its title and inspiration to art work by Steven Sorman.

"Quebrada" riffs off the word as defined in *Home Ground: Language for an American Landscape*, ed. Barry Lopez. San Antonio: Trinity University Press, 2006.

"Anti-Love Poem" takes off from a poem by Grace Paley.

"Elegy for Wilma" is for Clarice Geels.

"Until It Speaks" is dedicated to Marilyn Kallet.

Both "Near Paradise, Michigan" poems were inspired by photographs by Stan Krohmer.

The final line of "Poem Ending with a Line from Tranströmer" comes from Tomas Tranströmer's poem "Elegy."

"Wood Not Yet Out" was inspired by a poem by Alice Oswald.

"Olentangy Elegy" is for my sister Christina Clark.

"Cento" is a form of individual lines borrowed from other poets. Lines, in order, reference the following writers: Eamon Grennan, Sharon Olds, Alice Friman, Charles Wright, Alison Hawthorne Deming, A.R. Ammons, Louise Glück, Agha Shahid Ali, Victoria Chang, and D. Nurkse.

"Near the North Sea" borrows a number of details from a painting by Mathias J. Alten (1871–1938).

"Botanical Beliefs" is after a poem by Gerald Stern.

"Until It Speaks" and "If Riptides Were a Gateway" were both nominated for the 2012 Best of the Net Anthology; in addition, "If Riptides Were a Gateway" was also nominated for the Pushcart Prize.

Scandinavian Common Sense

Marie-France Raynault and Dominique Côté
in collaboration with Sébastien Chartrand

Scandinavian Common Sense

POLICIES TO TACKLE SOCIAL INEQUALITIES IN HEALTH

Baraka
Books
Montréal

LÉA·ROBACK
CENTRE DE RECHERCHE
SUR LES INÉGALITÉS SOCIALES
DE SANTÉ DE MONTRÉAL

This study was carried out by researchers at the Montreal-based Léa Roback Research Centre on Social Inequalities in Health and supported by a grant from the Canadian Institutes of Health Research. The Léa Roback Research Centre was financed by the Institute of Population and Public Health as part of the Canadian Institutes for Health Research's strategic initiative to create centres for research development.

ISBN 978-1-77186-064-2 pbk; 978-1-77186-065-9 epub; 978-1-77186-066-6 pdf; 978-1-77186-067-3 mobi/kindle

Cover by Folio infographie
Book design by Folio infographie

Legal Deposit. 4th quarter 2015
Bibliothèque et Archives nationales du Québec
Library and Archives Canada

Published by Baraka Books of Montreal.
6977. rue Lacroix
Montréal. Québec H4E 2V4
Telephone: 514 808-8504
info@barakabooks.com
www.barakabooks.com

Printed and bound in Quebec

We acknowledge the support from the Société de développement des entreprises culturelles (SODEC) and the Government of Quebec tax credit for book publishing administered by SODEC.

Société
de développement
des entreprises
culturelles
Québec

We acknowledge the support of the Canada Council for the Arts. which last year invested $153 million to bring the arts to Canadians throughout the country
Nous remercions le Conseil des arts du Canada de son soutien. L'an dernier. le Conseil a investi 153 millions de dollars pour mettre de l'art dans la vie des Canadiennes et des Canadiens de tout le pays.

Financé par le gouvernement du Canada
Funded by the Government of Canada | Canadä

ACKNOWLEDGMENTS

We would like to thank the experts with whom we have had the privilege of discussing Scandinavian policies and the complex questions to which they give rise. Henry Milner, a political scientist at the Université de Montréal and, for several years, a visiting professor at Umea University in Sweden, has been an extraordinary teacher over the years. Joakim Palme, a professor at the SOFI Centre of Stockholm University, and Irene Wennemo, formerly policies officer with the Swedish Trade Union Confederation, generously agreed to share their time and knowledge with us during interviews conducted in their country.

We thank Sébastien Chartrand, Ph.D., a researcher at the Léa Roback Centre, who co-wrote Chapter 8 while carrying out a field study on education in Sweden.

We are also grateful to the late Paul Bernard, the distinguished Université de Montréal sociologist, with whom this project began.

We thank, too, the Comprendre Montréal think tank, which helped us select for study those policies of most interest to Montreal-based decision-makers, as well as Isabelle Thérien for their invaluable help. Finally, we are grateful to Robin Philpot and Sean McCutcheon for their help with editing and translation.

CONTENTS

THE AUTHORS

Sébastien Chartrand (PhD Sociology) studied community organizations in Sweden at Stockholm University. He contributed to the evaluation of the community action policy of the Québec government along with Deena White from Université de Montréal. He participated in a study of community mobilization around school readiness in the Saint-Michel area for the Direction de santé publique de Montréal (Montreal public health department). He also worked as a research officer for the Lea Roback Research Center. He now teaches in Germany.

Dominique Côté (MA Sociology) has carried out research in social sciences for several years, mainly in the field of health and social services. She has contributed to the advancement of knowledge on different issues such as caregivers' needs, the impact of the shift to ambulatory care and women's occupational diseases. She is convinced of the great influence of policy choices on the everyday life and health of individuals. Her interest in the Nordic countries has not waned since she studied their family and work-life balancing policies for her Master's thesis. She is a research officer at the Lea Roback Research Centre.

Marie-France Raynault (MD, MSc Epidemiology, FRCP(c), FCAHS) is a medical doctor specialized in public health. She has been studying Swedish policies for many years and her expertise resulted in her being chosen by the Québec government to lead a study mission in Sweden to analyse its strategy to fight poverty. The results of her research guided the drafting of the *Act to combat poverty and social exclusion* (*Loi visant à lutter contre la pauvreté et l'exclusion sociale*). The act was unanimously adopted by the Québec Government in 2002. She now heads the Département de médecine préventive et santé publique (Preventive Medicine and Public Health Department) at the Centre hospitalier de l'Université de Montréal (University of Montreal Hospital Centre). She also heads the Lea Roback Research Centre, which she co-founded. Throughout her career, her main interest has been the health of the poor.

PREFACE TO THE ENGLISH EDITION

It is becoming increasingly clear that despite its impressive history of producing conceptual models and written documents about the importance of addressing social inequalities in health through public policy action, Canada does not do very well in implementing this vision. In contrast, the Nordic nations have achieved worldwide recognition for their success in building upon principles of human rights, social equity, and the importance of democratic participation to put into practice a wide range of public policies that promote the health and well-being of all of their residents. This excellent book provides an accessible but thorough overview of many of these public policy accomplishments.

These actions have taken place in the spheres of equitably distributing income and wealth, securing employment and improving workplace conditions, promoting early child development and family-friendly policies, assuring access to housing, education, and acting to improve gender equity and reduce social exclusion. In short, improving the quality and equitable distribution of the social determinants of health. As a result they have produced societies where economic and social security is provided to all of their members. Not surprisingly, they have also created societies where overall health is excellent and quality of life is high. The Nordic nations accomplish this at the same time as their economic performance in terms of economic growth and employment levels equals or out-performs Canada.

In addition to its thorough overview of equity-promoting public policy related to the important social determinants of health, the book's emphasis on the Nordic approach towards sustainable development is particularly innovative and useful. Nordic nations' efforts in this area are remarkable and closely related to their achievements in the other public policy areas detailed in this book. Environmental issues have generally been overlooked in analyses of how public policies can promote the health and well-being of the population in general and the vulnerable in particular.

The most striking conclusion to be drawn from this overview of public policy in the Nordic nations is that their governing authorities – with the full support and democratic participation of their public – believe in implementing public policies that improve rather than threaten the health and quality of life of their residents. They do this on the basis of the best available evidence and with a vision that asserts that even in an era of economic globalization, government, labour, business, and civil society can work together to improve the lives of people.

The vision of creating healthy and responsive societies is especially prominent in the Nordic nations, and this book does an excellent job of showing how to implement such a vision. I would note however that it is also present in the conservative nations of continental Europe where even without the strong historical influence of social democratic parties of the left, governments strive to promote the security and well-being of their members. It is a sad commentary that the public policy situation in Canada – e.g., growing income and wealth inequality, growth in precarious work, mediocre health and well-being of children, lack of national strategies for addressing food insecurity and housing insecurity, and consistently high and deepening levels of poverty – has fallen so far behind these other nations.

This excellent book seeks to rectify the Canadian situation by providing analysis of some of the macro-level factors shaping equity-promoting public policy in the Nordic nations such as intersectoral cooperation and the presence of proportional representation in the electoral process, meso-level descriptions of how Nordic nations develop and implement their public policies, and micro-level findings of the effects these public policies have on the population in general and the vulnerable in particular. It is thoughtful, comprehensive, and sure to enlighten.

While the provision of this information to Canadians will be absolutely essential in seeing its content applied to the Canadian scene, this will in itself not lead to the kinds of public policies necessary to promote Canadians' health and well-being. As demonstrated by the development and passage in Quebec of Bill 112, *Stratégie de lutte contre la pauvreté et l'exclusion sociale – Strategy against poverty and social exclusion* – what is required to bring on health supporting public policy is creation of a broad social movement that literally forces Canadian public policymakers to implement the kinds of reforms envisioned in this book.

There are reasons for optimism in this quest. Canadians are increasingly concerned about the growing social inequalities in their midst. Canadians also see a role for governmental action in addressing these inequalities. If and when Canadian policymakers come to agree that such actions are necessary, this volume will provide a road-map of how to proceed in this task. The authors and the Léa Roback Research Centre are to be commended for providing Canadians with such an excellent, thought-provoking, and hopefully action-provoking resource.

Dennis Raphael, PhD
Professor of Health Policy and Management,
York University, Toronto

PREFACE TO THE FIRST EDITION

Sweden and the other four Nordic countries (Denmark, Finland, Iceland and Norway) have implemented some of the most interesting examples of concrete policies to reduce social inequalities in health and to safeguard the well-being of vulnerable groups in our society. This book provides a comprehensive and insightful overview of many of the policies that have been introduced successfully over the years in one or several of the Nordic countries. By linking facts about the present status of social determinants to specific measures taken, the authors provide an instructive description of the actual effects and benefits of different social policies.

While every nation has its own political and cultural specificities we can learn from each other by sharing best practices. In particular, this applies to Canada and the Nordic countries that have a number of things in common, including mind-set, and whose societies are based on a similar set of basic values. Some of the measures taken by the Nordic countries may not be suitable in a different context and others may need to be adapted to local conditions. One also need remember that policies are not static and need to evolve over time. This includes social policies, where we have seen interesting developments in my own country in the last decade. Reforms have been introduced to safeguard the continued relevance and efficiency of the different social programs in a constantly changing society where public funds are not in abundance. I do believe, nevertheless, that many of the policies described in this book have the potential to serve as sources of inspiration and reference points for other countries like Canada.

Ottawa, 12 October 2012
Teppo Tauriainen
Ambassador of Sweden to Canada

INTRODUCTION

Income, social, and health inequalities often depend on decision-makers' choices and ideologies. These policy choices are based on knowledge and experience accumulated over the course of years in political, economic, social, and cultural contexts.

> The accumulating evidence concerning the impact upon health and well-being of broader determinants of health is available to policy makers in Canada, the U.S., the U.K., and Sweden. What is striking is the degree of variation in commitment to applying these findings across these nations.[1]

This work is an attempt to review, for the benefit of decision-makers, those public policies that have been most successful at reducing social inequalities and poverty. Numerous organizations have used a host of indices to compare countries in this respect. In the context of the struggle against social and health inequalities the example of the Nordic countries is particularly eloquent, for it shows the degree to which public policies really can positively affect an entire society.

The Nordic countries' decision-makers seem to have derived all the beneficial consequences from what is known about the impact of social determinants on health. These countries, which share the political principles and practices that comprise what is known as the Nordic model, are at the top when it comes to reducing human poverty. Over the course of decades, this model has acquired almost mythic status. It has allowed spectacular results to be attained in several sectors of social development. It has pushed back the limits of what social solidarity and state intervention can achieve.

---

1. Raphael, D., T. Bryant and M. Rioux. *Staying Alive: Critical Perspectives on Health, Illness, and Health Care*, Canadian Scholars' Press, Toronto, 2006, 1st edition, page 364.

The Nordic countries were pioneers, and they remain today a part of the world well worth looking at, a vast and unique laboratory for experiments in governance. The small size of these countries, which favours experiments, surely has something to do with this. As well, they remain a source of inspiration because of the richness of their political history, their populations' consensus support for state intervention and their solidarity on social and ecological issues, and because their political class continues to prioritize the common good.

Even if the Nordic model, whose social policies are typically generous, has undergone major changes, the governments of the Nordic countries still develop equity policies that differ from those of other Western countries in their breadth and in their aims of equity, while continuing to maintain a high level of economic competitiveness. Buhigas Schubert and Martens explain this convincingly:

> Nordic societies started doing their homework before many others in Europe, recognising the need to adapt to global competition while at the same time maintaining the welfare state as the essential element of the system – and not even putting it up for discussion. In other words, the transformation needed for successful integration into a globalised economy has not been achieved by cutting welfare, but rather through collective commitment, a vision of the value of investing in high standards, and a willingness to pay for it.[2]

Even the ways of orchestrating political responses to global economic changes show, at least in the case of Sweden, the continuing existence of a Nordic political process, from which one can also draw inspiration:

> The economic recovery was to be the proof of the greatness — in the largest sense of the term — of the Swedish model: trusting relations at all levels of society, a developed feeling among social partners of responsibility, sociological proximity between the political class and the citizens, the limited nature of social cleavages and the strength of the bonds of solidarity, transparency and effectiveness of the bureaucracy... All these factors gave Swedish society its capacity to react rapidly and in a determined fashion, when others were bogged down in insurmountable conflicts of interest.[3]

---

2. Buhigas Schubert, C. and H. Martens. *The Nordic model: A recipe for European success?* European Policy Centre, Brussels, 2005, p. 109.
3. Kalinowski, W. Pourquoi les Suédois ont-ils des raisons de s'inquiéter. 2006. [www.lavie-desidees.fr/Pourquoi-les-Suedois-ont-ils-des.html. Accessed Feb 6, 2014], free translation.

The WHO's Commission on Social Determinants of Health has clearly described the social and political conditions that favour health. One can easily recognize in these descriptions the public policies of the Nordic countries. We have highlighted the common characteristics of the policies that have helped make Nordic societies environments that are fair, and that favour health for the greatest number of people.

Research of use to decision-makers

The research that led to the publication of this work was carried out by the Montreal-based Léa Roback Research Centre on Social Inequalities in Health.

The centre was created in response to a call for proposals from the Canadian Institutes of Health Research, for creating centres for research into the health effects of physical and social milieus. The researchers at the Léa Roback Centre focus on the main determinants of social inequalities in health, and on interventions likely to reduce these inequalities. It includes researchers from Montreal universities and from public health organizations. The centre's researchers carry out studies in the greater Montreal region and interact with local and regional decision-makers in provincial ministries, in municipal government, and in a number of other organizations. The centre's mission is to produce research results of use to decision-makers, and gives rise to numerous initiatives to exchange knowledge with them.

The choice of studying the Nordic countries

Very few studies have evaluated public policies. As a general rule, governmental interventions or policies are not implemented using a scientific method (i.e., with an experimental and a control group), thus allowing their consequences and effectiveness to be measured. Our study, therefore, focused on the countries that have clearly succeeded in reducing social inequalities. These successes are documented by data and reports from major international organizations such as the United Nations (UN) and the Organization for Economic Cooperation and Development (OECD), as well as by experts on public health and on social inequalities.

The Nordic countries were chosen as the object of this study because, when countries are ranked by how well they fight social inequalities, they are at the top of the list. The countries we chose are Sweden, Norway,

Denmark, and Finland. We excluded Iceland; with only 330,000 inhabitants, it is a small state and cannot be compared with Quebec. The other Nordic countries have geographic, demographic, and cultural realities – such as remote regions and a low population density – close to the Quebec context. For the very same reasons, we have excluded a comparison with Japan, which also does well on indicators of social equity and health.

Aim and target audience

In the light of hard data about the Nordic countries' success, the prime goal of this work is to make known the best practices, highlighting inspiring examples.

In keeping with the Léa Roback Centre's mission of exchanging knowledge, decision-makers and students comprise the main target audiences for this work. This is why, for each of the themes studied, we explain not only the main policy thrusts but we also (in the sections headed 'Key ideas') give examples of concrete interventions, illustrating how policies play out in people's daily lives.

This research project was planned so as to inform those who design and make decisions about policies for application in urban milieus. Our results will also be of interest to anyone working at improving social equity and the health and well-being of populations. Policies are presented concisely so as not to burden the text with detail. The exhaustive bibliography at the end of the work will allow the reader to find not only the original texts of policies, but also studies and syntheses by outside observers.

Methodology

We met individually with Montreal-based decision-makers who collaborate with the Léa Roback Centre to delimit the domains and themes to examine in this survey. Exchanging knowledge with decision-makers is part of the mission of the Léa Roback Centre. These discussions allowed us to define the several fields of interest that have guided our research.

The literature about the policies of Nordic countries that could help in reducing both social inequalities in health and poverty in urban and near-urban areas was chosen, analysed, and summarized. Four types of data sources were used: scientific articles describing or evaluating policies; websites of the governments of the countries studied, of ministries, agencies, municipalities, and organizations such as the Swedish Institute, Statistics

Norway, or the Finnish National Board of Education; publications by the governments of the countries studied, such as annual reports, documents on policies, etc., (and, when necessary, direct communications with government agents); and data and publications from major international organizations such as the European Union, the Council of Europe, the European Parliament, the OECD, the United Nations Development Programme (UNDP), UNICEF, UNESCO, and the Nordic Council. We also made use of information from other international organizations such as Eurocities, the network of the 130 largest cities in Europe.

We have compiled the most recent data available using the following criteria for inclusion: symmetry with selected countries in the selected policy fields; the evaluative and instructive nature of the data; and promising practices or practices that have proven their efficacy and exemplify typical Nordic ways of doing things. We excluded epistemological studies concerned with theoretical debates rather than concrete policies.

It should be noted that a great deal of the information here comes from Sweden. The Swedish government translates a mass of documents about its policies: national reports, legal texts, working documents, information sheets for the general public, and most ministries' and government agencies' websites. The other Nordic countries also translate their documentation, but in a less systematic fashion. Moreover, Sweden and the other Nordic countries share a very similar social-protection system. The main lines of the policies of Sweden often converge with those of Norway, Denmark or Finland, and this is particularly so for social policies such as gender equity, income security, family policies or housing assistance. Though there are notable differences between the choices the Nordic countries make in concretely applying policies to protect their citizens, the goals and the means they use are so similar that scientific observers have concluded that the Nordic model, which this work will describe, really exists.

To conclude, it should be noted that the group of Nordic countries differs from the group of Scandinavian countries. Strictly speaking, the Scandinavian group is defined by common linguistic roots, and includes Norway, Sweden, Denmark, and Iceland. Finnish, a Finno-Ugric language, shares common roots with Hungarian, and is very distinct from the Scandinavian languages. The group of Nordic countries, therefore, includes Scandinavia and Finland. Note that Finland was part of Sweden until the beginning of the twentieth century, and a non-negligible proportion of its citizens speak Swedish, and are hence Scandinavian.

This survey of documentation on the Nordic countries provides a journey into the heart of the policies of Sweden, Norway, Denmark, and Finland. It is our hope that this journey will strike a spark, that you will discover that there exists in the north of Europe a world of possibilities and well-governed societies.

CHAPTER 1

Social Inequalities in Health:
a Real and Persistent Problem

The existence of social inequalities in health is now recognized as a very real and world-wide problem. Whitehead and Dahlgren (2006) have defined such inequalities as "systematic differences in health between different socioeconomic groups within a society."[1] As well as factors such as age, sex, genes, and the risks of exposure to an infectious disease, there are also systematic determinants of health. These are socially produced and avoidable.

Obvious links

The links between the social dimension and health are striking. There is generally a correlation between socioeconomic status and life expectancy at all levels of the social hierarchy. In other words, all social classes are affected, even those that are not disadvantaged. This is shown in Figure 1.1, in which socioeconomic status is indicated by professional category.

A difference between average life expectancies can also be observed at the neighbourhood scale. The difference in average life expectancy between the poorest Montreal neighbourhoods, located in the southeast of the island, and the richest, in the west, is striking: six years for men, four years for women.

The phenomenon is universal. Observed health-related differences are not randomly distributed in the population. They vary, following a

---

1. Whitehead M. and G. Dahlgren (2006). *Levelling up (part 1): a discussion paper on concepts and principles for tackling social inequities in health*, Copenhagen, WHO Collaborating Centre for Policy Research on Social Determinants of Health, University of Liverpool, pages 14-15.

FIGURE 1.1

Occupational class differences in life expectancy.
England and Wales, 1997-1999

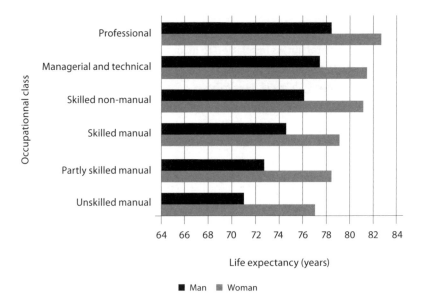

Life expectancy (years)

■ Man   ■ Woman

Source: Reprinted from *Social Determinants of Health: The Solid Facts*, 2nd edition, by Richard Wilkinson and Michael Marmot, p. 10, 2003.

systematic, recurrent, and predictable pattern, as a function of socio-economic groups. The World Health Organization (WHO) study on the social determinants of health confirms this: "In countries at all levels of income, health and illness follow a social gradient: the lower the socio-economic position, the worse the health."[2]

This model is global, though its importance varies from country to country. Some countries succeed in reducing these inequalities. In doing so, as a general rule, society as a whole benefits, for though the health of an individual varies as a function of socioeconomic status, the average health of all the inhabitants of a developed country varies not as a function of

2. WHO Commission on Social Determinants of Health. *Closing the gap in a generation: Health equity through action on the social determinants of health*, World Health Organization, Geneva, 2008, page vi.

average income but of inequalities. The more the gap between rich and poor is reduced, the better the average health of the population. As figure 1.2 illustrates, this is particularly true for mental health.

FIGURE 1.2

Prevalence in mental illness in relation to income inequality among rich countries

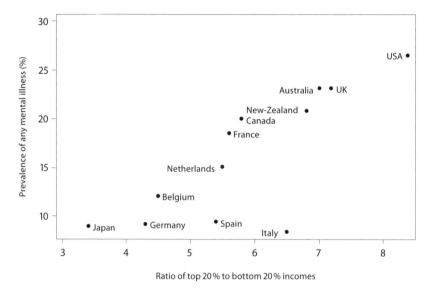

Source: Reprinted with the permission of Elservier, "The problems of relative deprivation: Why some societies do better than others," by R. Wilkinson and K. Pickett, in *Social Science & Medicine*, Vol. 65, p. 1968, 2007.

Some hypotheses on causality of poverty and illness

In recent years, several researchers have been investigating the biological mechanisms by which poverty leads to poor health. Though still fairly young, this is a promising field; researchers have uncovered interesting lines of enquiry and formulated hypotheses that merit investigation. It is generally acknowledged that poor health can drag a person down to an unenviable socioeconomic situation (though social mechanisms such as disability insurance and health insurance can largely attenuate this decline.) It is also acknowledged that, inversely, poverty can affect health. To better understand the relationship between poverty and poor health, we present here some of the physio-pathologic mechanisms discussed in the recent scientific literature.

Depression and mental health

Numerous studies have established a link between depression and poverty. The physiological mechanisms involved depend mainly on excessive secretion of stress hormones.

Chronic stress, such as that provoked by a prolonged state of poverty, leads to high levels of cortisol. These high levels block the action of the receptors in the brain whose function is to respond to the flux of neurotransmitters activated by the perceived need to react to stress or danger. The response normally ordered by the brain in reaction to a threat, problem, or any troubling situation is to fight or fly, after which the level of cortisol comes back to normal. But when cortisol levels remain high, brain chemistry is impaired. In short, high levels of stress hormones inhibit action, and a prolonged state of inhibition encourages the development of a state of depression.

Depression and a diverse range of mental health problems are more prevalent among the socially or economically disadvantaged. Poverty also impacts mental health through impairing physical health and childhood development. "Mental health problems are not randomly distributed in society, and if the epidemiological data indicate that one person in four is likely to suffer a mental health problem during his or her lifetime, it is not just any 'one person in four'."[3] Inequalities in mental health reflect existing divisions in society: divisions of class, sex, age, and ethnic origin. Inequalities exist not only in the distribution of mental health problems, but also in the social factors that cause these problems and in those that facilitate recovery. Access to resources and services that help prevent or treat these problems also depends on socioeconomic inequalities. Noteworthy among other possible causal mechanisms of mental illness are social exclusion, isolation, and privation, which are both causes and consequences of such illness.

---

3. *"Les problèmes de santé mentale ne sont pas distribués de façon aléatoire dans la société, et si les données épidémiologiques révèlent qu'une personne sur quatre est susceptible de souffrir d'un problème de santé mentale au cours de sa vie, ce n'est pas n'importe quelle «une personne sur quatre."* Deplanche, F. and L. Fournier. *Surveillance des inégalités sociales de santé: Indicateurs de santé mentale – Rapport final.* Centre de recherche Léa-Roback sur les inégalités sociales de santé, Montreal, 2011, p. 31.

To reduce social inequalities in mental health, public policy should, of course, involve direct investment in mental and physical health. But, as well, we have to grapple with economic disadvantage and, above all, with job status. Furthermore, it is essential that investments be made to increase social capital and support individuals.

Cardiovascular disease

Poverty during childhood affects physical health not only when children are young but also when they become adults. A growing body of scientific data on the life course demonstrates that the health status observed at any time is markedly determined by the cumulative effect of preceding circumstances. The study of the life course and accumulated vulnerabilities, which some authors consider fundamental to understanding the origins of social inequalities in health, supports the thesis that such inequalities stem from the conditions of the first years of development.

A relationship can thus be observed between poverty in infancy and cardiovascular disease in adulthood, even taking account of socioeconomic status in adulthood. Atherosclerosis, the slow and progressive formation of plaques in the arteries, can begin in childhood. This condition is strongly associated with poor nutrition which, in turn, is more common in underprivileged neighbourhoods. Moreover, excess weight and obesity are associated with poverty and food insufficiency, that is, the uncertain or limited availability of nutritious foods. These conditions are important risk factors for cardiovascular disease. Unfortunately, they are observed more and more often in children, and at increasingly younger ages. In Great Britain, poverty has been linked to obesity in children as young as five years old.

The endocrine and immune systems

Over time, the stress engendered by chronic poverty raises the production of stress hormones such as cortisol to unhealthy levels, and does so repeatedly, almost constantly. An elevated level of stress hormones harms the mechanisms by which the organism defends itself in the short and the long term from diseases. We know, for example, that an elevated level of cortisol reduces the number of lymphocytes (immune system cells) in the blood. Globally, excessive production of stress hormones such as adrenaline, noradrenaline, and cortisol (produced by the adrenal glands) affects the functional capacity of immune cells. This, in turn, reduces the capacity to resist the infections and other diseases against which the immune system normally fights.

The human brain reacts to acute stress, traditionally a threat to survival, by adaptive 'fight or flight' physiological responses triggered by massive secretions into the blood of stress hormones which, once the stress has passed, quickly drop back to their initial level. Poverty, however, with its daily frustrations and omnipresent insecurity, induces a state of chronic stress.

These physiological effects of stress are felt even by children. As Dr. Louise Séguin explains: "Children as well as parents experience poverty. The stress experienced by the child is reflected by an elevated level of cortisol which affects the child's immune system, physiological functioning, brain, and development."[4] Moreover, numerous studies confirm the finding that poor children have higher rates of poor health than children in general. Poor mothers more frequently report that their children have average or poor health, or have been hospitalized. They also report a larger number of health problems, including problems associated with the immune system, even in infants. At the age of two, poor children are more likely to suffer several health problems at the same time, an indication that their immune system may be weakened by long-term stress. We also know that chronic as compared to short-term poverty has greater impact on the health of children.

Cognitive development

Socioeconomic status does not only affect health directly. It also, though indirectly, affects cognitive development. During infancy the brain develops by mechanisms, such as blood irrigation and the formation of neural connections, whose normal operation depends on an optimal physiological state. In children of poor families, elevated levels of stress hormones inhibit both synaptic connections between neurons and blood supply to the brain. The following extract from a *Financial Times* interview with Dr. Jack Shonkoff, a specialist in childhood development, summarizes the

---

4. "*La pauvreté est vécue par l'enfant comme par les parents. Le stress vécu par l'enfant se reflète par un taux de cortisol élevé, qui affecte son système immunitaire, son fonctionnement physiologique, son cerveau et ses capacités de développement.*" Cited in Observatoire montréalais des inégalités sociales et de la santé (OMISS), "*La pauvreté des enfants au Québec a des impacts évidents sur leur santé: 41 % plus d'hospitalisation chez les enfants pauvres.*" Press release for the OMISS colloquium "Pauvreté et Santé des Enfants," June 1, 2006.

problem well. "Many children growing up in very poor families with low social status experience unhealthy levels of stress hormones, which impair their neural development. That effect is on top of any damage caused by inadequate nutrition and exposure to environmental toxins."[5]

The last UNICEF report on childhood poverty (2012) also makes this association between disadvantage in childhood and health in adulthood, while also painting a global portrait of the repercussions of childhood poverty on a society as a whole.

> [F]ailure to protect children from poverty is one of the most costly mistakes a society can make. The heaviest cost of all is borne by the children themselves. But their nations must also pay a very significant price – in reduced skills and productivity, in lower levels of health and educational achievement, in increased likelihood of unemployment and welfare dependence, in the higher costs of judicial and social protection systems, and in the loss of social cohesion.[6]

In its report on the situation of young people in Montreal, the city's Direction de santé publique (Department of Public Health) states that all children do not arrive at school with the same advantages and that the school milieu presents several hurdles for the most disadvantaged children. When cognitive development, skills acquisition, and academic learning have been impeded, it becomes more difficult to escape the poverty in which one grew up. After failing in school, young people tend to drop out, become parents prematurely, and reproduce the difficult conditions they have known since their childhood, with all the familiar negative impacts on health. From infancy to adulthood, they encounter situations and circumstances that degrade their health: academic difficulties, poor training during adolescence, jobs with poor working conditions and inadequate income, low-grade housing, and more.

Early intervention is needed to counter the impacts of poverty on cognitive development. In this context, the index of school readiness is a valuable tool. It is used to assess a child's degree of preparedness even before the child starts going to school. The index measures a child's development in five domains: cognitive and linguistic development; communication

---

5. Cookson, Clive. "Poverty mars formation of infant brains." *Financial Times,* Feb 16, 2008.

6. UNICEF. Measuring child poverty: new league tables of child poverty in the world's richest countries. *Innocenti Report Card 10,* UNICEF Innocenti Research Center, Florence, 2012, p. 2.

skills and general knowledge; social competence; affective maturity; and physical health and well-being.

Montreal's Direction de santé publique has conducted a survey to measure school readiness on its territory, and to determine what is needed to ensure that all children are ready for schooling. The results showed that the proportion of vulnerable children (that is, those assessed as deficient in at least one domain) rose from 28 percent in neighbourhoods with a 10 percent poverty rate to 40 percent in those with a 52 percent poverty rate.

Illnesses associated with atmospheric pollution

It has been clearly shown that low socioeconomic status is associated with greater exposure to pollution and its trail of health problems. It suffices to think of the poor air quality in working-class neighbourhoods that are near highways or industrial zones. Such neighbourhoods, moreover, are often far from parks and open green spaces where vegetation helps purify the air. Numerous studies have shown that as air pollution increases, so too does the frequency of hospitalizations for respiratory problems. A Montreal study has shown that people who live near roads with heavy traffic are at increased risk of being hospitalized for respiratory problems; and 1,500 premature deaths per year in Montreal are attributable to atmospheric pollution.

The fine particles in the air that cause certain health problems can enter the body not only through respiratory pathways but also through blood vessels, and hence the hypothesis that fine particles (less than 2.5 μm in diameter) are inhaled, pass through the tissues of the respiratory system to penetrate into blood vessels, and thus encourage the development of atherosclerosis (plaques that block arteries and may cause cardiovascular diseases such as strokes, infarctions, and angina). One of the many studies supporting this hypothesis compared data from 51 American cities. When all other risk factors for mortality had been taken into account, life expectancy dropped by 0.6 years for each incremental increase in fine particle concentration of ten micrograms per cubic meter of air. This effect was largely attributable to cardiovascular failure. And since pollution levels between cities can vary by as much as 20 μg/m³, life expectancy varies even more…

Upstream: the social determinants of health

The negative repercussions of poverty on health mentioned above give only a sampling of the effects of poverty on the health and well-being of individuals. There are, in fact, many other such effects. These include, to name a few, diabetes, cancer, infectious diseases, nicotine addiction, respiratory diseases, intrauterine retardation, and accidental injury of children. The prevalence of these health problems is higher amongst disadvantaged people.

Upstream of the physiological mechanisms triggered by poverty are what are known as the social determinants of health. This term refers to poor living conditions imposed by poverty, which also constitute risk factors, such as unhealthy housing, lack of education, poor working conditions, limited access to quality food, and weak social support. As well as such directly operating living conditions, the social determinants also include more global realities such as, for example, government policies (access to education, universality of healthcare, family benefits, access to housing, etc.), ethnic discrimination, and the economic situation. The diagram below (Figure 1.3), prepared by the WHO Commission on Social Determinants, clearly illustrates the different types of determinants and the steps in the process by which they produce social inequalities in health.

FIGURE 1.3

Commission on Social Determinants of Health conceptual framework

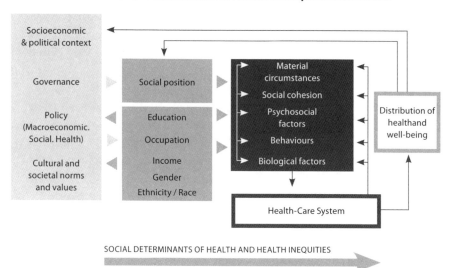

Source: Commission on Social Determinants of Health (2008). Amended from Solar & Irwin. 2007.

This diagram highlights the avoidable nature of these inequalities, and shows the consequences of political and economic choices.

Several dimensions, approaches, and models intersect in analyses of the causes of social inequalities in health. Psychosocial, behavioural or cultural models, the life-course approach, the materialist model — all refer to different aspects of the phenomenon, which can play a role to varying degrees, according to the situation. Several elements are at work in situations of poverty. These include increased exposure to health risks such as stress (psychosocial model); the adoption of harmful behaviours because of their predominance in the social environment (behavioural and cultural models); an accumulation of circumstances during the course of life that weaken health (life-course approach); or a lack of money to pay for needed resources and services (materialist model). All are social causes of health inequalities.

A global trend

The OECD has now confirmed that, over the last thirty years, the income gap between rich and poor has been steadily increasing not only in most of its member countries, but also in several developing countries. Moreover, wealth-distribution mechanisms (income taxes, social transfers, etc.) are decreasing in efficiency, particularly in Canada. According to Angel Gurria, Secretary-General of the OECD, the observed trend refutes the hypothesis that, without any state intervention, profits from economic growth will end up profiting all, since the income gaps have grown during a long period of economic growth.

Between 1979 and 2005, well before the 2008 economic crisis, the income of our richest American neighbours increased by 228 percent while that of the poorest increased by only six percent. Not since 1929 has there been such concentration at the top level of income distribution. Between 2004 and 2005, in this country, after-tax incomes rose by $180,000 for the richest one percent of households, by $400 for the middle class, and by $200 for low-income households.

Widening gaps in Canada

The gap between rich and poor has grown large in Canada but, after tax and social transfers, the range of the income spectrum is not as wide as in the United States. Though the situation in Canada is less extreme thanks to social programs, it is nonetheless similar. In recent years, for the first time in the history of Canada, the rich have, in effect, appropriated much of the profits from growth. Between 1950 and 1960, the richest one percent of the population benefitted from eight percent of the total increase in income. Between 1997 and 2007, this percentage increased to 32 percent. The result: in 2007, 10 percent of Canadians earned 41 percent of income before taxes and 90 percent of their co-citizens shared the remaining 59 percent.

Between 1948 and 2009, the tax rate on the highest-income earners dropped from 80 percent to 42.9 percent. Taking into account all fiscal measures (taxes on income, capital gains, consumption, and property, and corporate income taxes), between 1990 and 2005, income taxes and other taxes for those among the richest one percent of Canadians decreased twice more than for average Canadians. In 2005, the rich even enjoyed a taxation rate slightly lower than that imposed on the poorest 10 percent of taxpayers. Statistics Canada estimates that between 1989 and 2007, after-tax income grew 7.6 percent for the lowest quintile and 30 percent for the highest quintile. Since the end of the 1970s, incomes have doubled for the richest one percent, tripled for the richest 0.1 percent, and quintupled for the richest 0.01 percent. The result: in 2009, only 3.8 percent of Canadians owned 67 percent of all financial wealth.

According to the OECD, the gaps have been widened, at least in part, by cuts in the government social programs that redistribute some of the wealth created and by cuts in the taxes imposed on the wealthy. Canada can be distinguished from other countries by the erosion of its redistribution measures. Formerly, taxes and social programs in Canada succeeded in checking at least 70 percent of intrinsic market inequalities. But, since the 1980s, cuts in social programs (employment insurance, transfers, social insurance) and cuts in taxes, especially in taxes on the rich, have reduced the state's counterbalancing effect to less than 40 percent. Today, Canada compensates inequalities less than do the majority of other OECD countries. Moreover, in a comparison of the 34 OECD member countries, with a rank of one indicating the best performing country, Canada ranks number 22 for childhood poverty and number 21 for poverty of the entire population. In 2012, UNICEF compared childhood poverty across 35 countries. Canada ranked number 24 (and Iceland, with a childhood poverty rate of less than five percent, ranked number one).

The Conference Board of Canada evaluated poverty in a group of seventeen developed countries. Canada was near the bottom of the list: in fifteenth place for poverty among the working-age population — only the United States and Japan have higher poverty rates — and in thirteenth place for childhood poverty. Poverty has increased between the mid-1990s and the mid-2000s from 12.8 percent to 15.1 percent among children, from 9.4 percent to 12.2 percent among the working-age population, and from 2.9 percent to 5.9 percent among the elderly.

The situation in Quebec

The trend toward wealth concentration is more marked in English Canada than in Quebec. This difference might be explained by the fact that a larger portion of the income of the rich now comes from salaries, and salary increases are more subject to American influence in English Canada than in Quebec. Anglophone employers must compete with their US counterparts so as not to lose good candidates. The francophone market is different, for French-speaking candidates, it seems, are less inclined to leave their country for one with a different language and culture.

But Quebec has also been able to differentiate itself from the rest of the country by doing better at distributing wealth than the other provinces. UNICEF has emphasized this:

> The results [of provincial strategies to reduce poverty] in Quebec, among the first to set targets to reduce poverty and implement changes, have been positive. Quebec is the province where the rate of child poverty is lowest, as compared to the broader provincial population. [...] Quebec is one of only two Canadian provinces where the child poverty rate is slightly lower than that of the broader provincial population...[7]

The gaps have widened over several decades but, since the mid-1990s, the percentage of the population of Quebec that is poor, after taxes (measured by the Low Income Measure) has dropped slightly, going from 11.0 percent in 1997 to 9.3 percent in 2010. In Canada, from 1996 to 2008 the percentage of poor families and individuals (as measured by the after-tax Low Income Measure) has remained stable at 15.1 percent.

The specter of inequality, nonetheless, is looming larger in Quebec. There is a striking disparity between the Montreal region and the rest of the province. The poverty rate (measured by the personal after-tax Low Income

---

7. *UNICEF Report Card 10: Measuring Child Poverty, Canadian Companion,* 2010, pp. 1 and 5.

Measure, 2010) in the Montreal region is 16.6 percent, far higher than that for the province as a whole (9.3 percent). According to the Direction de santé publique de Montréal: "in 2005, low-income families with children from 0 to 5 years old were three times more numerous in Montreal than in the rest of Quebec; and families with young children that receive social assistance were twice as numerous here."[8]

Possible solutions

Socioeconomic inequalities are on the rise everywhere in the world. This can be avoided. To do so, the OECD proposes solutions that call upon governments to return to more progressive taxes and larger social investments, particularly in the education sector. "Any policy strategy to reduce the growing divide between rich and poor should rest on three main pillars: more intensive human capital investment; inclusive employment promotion; and well-designed tax/transfer redistribution policies."[9]

One logic is as follows: the best way to reduce inequalities rests in the development of a greater number of good jobs and this requires improved training for workers. Education, from childhood to adulthood, and continued training after that, are crucial.

UNICEF considers that childhood poverty is avoidable in the rich countries, because it depends in large part on government policies, and notably on the importance accorded to child benefits and tax credits.

Until the mid-1990s, thanks to its fiscal system and social transfers, Canada succeeded as well as the Nordic countries in rebalancing inequalities. Cuts in means-tested benefits (benefits for individuals with financial resources below a certain threshold) are largely responsible for the subsequent failure to rebalance inequalities, along with smaller transfer payments and less targeted programs. Changes in the tax system also played a role. Some OECD countries are now thinking of restoring tax rates on the richest to high levels, given that these rich now have more capacity to pay than before. This, clearly, is an example Canada should follow.

---

8. *"[E]n 2005, par comparaison avec le reste du Québec, les familles à faible revenu et ayant des enfants de 0 à 5 ans étaient trois fois plus nombreuses à Montréal. On y trouvait deux fois plus de familles avec de jeunes enfants prestataires de l'aide sociale."* Direction de santé publique de l'Agence de la santé et des services sociaux de Montréal. *Rapport du directeur de santé publique 2011 – Les inégalités sociales de santé à Montréal. Le chemin parcouru*, Montréal, 2011, rapport synthèse, p. 8.
9. OECD. *Divided We Stand: Why Inequality Keeps Rising*, 2011, p. 4.

CHAPTER 2

The Best Strategies for Reducing Social Inequalities in Health

Social inequalities in health may now be clearly recognized, but this is not true of strategies for reducing them. Such reduction strategies draw on many areas of interventions and challenge policies in a wide range of sectors, including education, housing, sustainable development, and health services. Article 54 of Quebec's Public Health Act already allows evaluation of the anticipated health impacts of any law or policy proposed by the government. Health Impact Assessment, an evaluation method developed in the United Kingdom, can be used to help design effective interventions aimed at reducing social health inequalities.

The following pages describe two pioneering initiatives aimed at reducing social inequalities in health: the Dutch national research program and the WHO Commission on Social Determinants of Health. Finally, a reflection on the role of sustainable development will inform this study of Nordic policies for reducing social inequalities in health.

The Netherlands' program of studies

The Dutch national research program on interventions aimed at reducing social inequalities in health has carried out an ambitious study. After evaluating different kinds of interventions, policies, and programs, the research team presented them for review to experts and practitioners in a wide range of domains — academia, public policy (former ministers, for example), health promotion, working conditions, housing conditions, income, education, health services — and to politicians spanning the entire political spectrum. The reviewers were asked to assess the feasibility and efficacy of the various strategies. The study's conclusions have been adopted in the work of the WHO and that of research teams in various countries. The four 'winning' strategies are presented in order of priority in the diagram below (Figure 2.1).

FIGURE 2.1

Strategies to reduce the effects of poverty on health

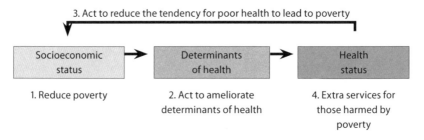

Source: Reprinted from Smith. R. "Countering child poverty," *British Medical Journal* (322): 1137–1138, 2001, with permission from BMJ Publishing Group Ltd.

The Erasmus University study team concluded that the most effective strategy for reducing problems of health and mortality flowing from social inequalities is to act at the source, investing to prevent and reduce poverty. According to the diagram by Stronks, republished by Smith, intervention on root causes is more effective and less costly than assuming the burden of health problems.

The Dutch team compared the first strategy — programs of social protection and wealth redistribution — with the second — interventions to reduce the exposure of disadvantaged persons to the intermediate determinants of health problems such as poor housing and nicotine addiction. Such interventions, targeted at health determinants, are less effective than those that directly address socioeconomic status.

The third strategy was to minimize the effects of poor health on social mobility. Concrete examples of what this means included offering special help at school to kids suffering from health problems affecting their academic performance, and increasing the participation of handicapped people in the job market by adapting workplaces to their needs. Decent income security benefits for those who are out of work could also reduce the impact of poor health on their socioeconomic status. According to Mackenbach, principal investigator of the Dutch team, this strategy, though promising, is little used.

Finally, the fourth and least effective strategy is to offer supplementary health services to those whose health has been weakened during years of privation. For example, this strategy could mean providing access to doctors who are aware of the problems of poverty so that patients could rapidly be referred to professionals in the social services.

Concretely, according to the researchers, the priorities in improving socioeconomic status are education and better work conditions and income for those at the bottom of the social hierarchy.

The WHO experts who studied the social determinants of health agree: "Good health involves reducing levels of educational failure, reducing insecurity and unemployment, and improving housing standards. Societies that enable all citizens to play a full and useful role in the social, economic and cultural life of their society will be healthier than those where people face insecurity, exclusion and deprivation." [1]

The WHO Commission on Social Determinants of Health

The WHO Commission on Social Determinants of Health assembled dozens of scientists from all the continents to study the social determinants of health. The commission's conclusions are based mainly on the final reports produced by nine knowledge networks. The international experts who made up these groups collated the results from the most recent studies on the following themes: early childhood development, employment conditions, social exclusion, globalization, health systems, priority public health conditions, measurement and evidence, women and gender equity, and urbanization. This work led to the publication of a major report, *Closing the gap in a generation: Health equity through action on the social determinants of health*, which confirms the strategies chosen by the Dutch team. The WHO report deals with the macroeconomic and structural dimensions of social inequalities in health while also dealing in detail with specific sectors of intervention.

---

1. Wilkinson, R. and M. Marmot (eds.). *Social Determinants of Health — The Solid Facts.* World Health Organization, Copenhagen, 2004, p. 11.

"Tackle the inequitable distribution of power, money and resources"[2]

To really succeed in curbing inequalities, one has to act on the roots of social and economic structures, targeting not only the redistribution of wealth and resources, but also the redistribution of power. This is mainly a question of maximizing the capacities of individuals to control their lives. The report proposes tackling the inequalities inherent in social structures, such as gender inequity. For this purpose, a committed, adequately financed, and legitimized public sector is essential. Similarly, civil society needs significant space, good support, and broad credibility. The report encourages the development of a responsible private sector in a society in which collective action and the public interest are valued.

The report's strategies — which can also be considered objectives — may, at first view, seem idealistic and unattainable. Yet there are countries that succeed in working towards these goals, hence the interest in studying the many mechanisms that have been implemented to assure democratic life and truly universal access to resources.

"Improve daily living conditions"[3]

Reducing inequalities also means acting directly on the social determinants of health, either by countering their harmful effects or by preventing exposure to them. As we know, the most effective interventions are preventive measures acting on the roots of problems. It is no surprise, therefore, that such measures are needed from the time of birth on. This is why the WHO Commission stresses the importance of birth circumstances and maternal health, and of investing first in early childhood development and later in education. The Commission also stresses the importance of living and working conditions, as well as of social protection measures providing a financial cushion in cases of hard knocks or at certain stages of life; for example, on losing a job, becoming sick, or going back to school, or on the occasion of the birth of a child or the breakup of a marriage.

When it comes to improving daily living conditions, the Nordic countries stand out. This is no accident: investments in the common good

---

2. Commission on the Social Determinants of Health (2008). Closing the gap in a generation; Final report, page 2.
3. Ibid.

and in social solidarity are viewed very positively in these countries and, moreover, these investments are substantial and made in key fields such as early childhood development (daycares with high-quality programs and well-trained educators), education (free schooling at any stage in life), and social protection (measures of balancing work and family, state-funded alimony, reintegration into the workplace, etc.)

"Measure and understand the problem and assess the impact of action"[4]

One of the three overarching recommendations made in the Commission's report is to evaluate the possible impact of all major policy changes on the health of underprivileged people. This recommendation, which affects such domains as education, employment, income, and social security, also figures in the study by Mackenbach's team mentioned above. The two other recommendations made in the Commission's report are to monitor social inequalities in health and measure their evolution in the population so as to gather the data needed to inform the choice of actions to take; and to monitor the evolution of the social determinants of health, train political decision-makers and healthcare practitioners, and perform more research on the social determinants of health.

The Nordic countries are notable, once again, for their well established tradition of evaluating the effects of their programs and basing political decisions on convincing data, or on the results of commissions of enquiry or of scientific research carried out specifically to elucidate questions being debated.

Because of their scope and scientific quality, the studies carried out in the Netherlands and those of the Commission on the Social Determinants of Health provide a very good and up-to-date overview of what is known about means of reducing social inequalities in health. Their conclusions build upon those of the first major studies on the subject such as the Black Report, the Whitehead Report, and the Acheson Report. Since these reports were published, more recent studies have corroborated the conclusions, made by the Dutch national research program and the Commission on social determinants of health, about the most important interventions: tackling the root causes of social inequalities in health (poverty, the income gap between rich and poor, education); reducing socio-economic gaps from

---

4. Ibid.

childhood on by investing in infants; providing social protection at various stages in life; and compensating for the effects of being disadvantaged by means of targeted services and measures.

The role of policy in reducing poverty

Of all the strategies proposed for reducing social inequalities, state interventions to decrease poverty are essential and determinant. UNICEF measures their effectiveness as follows:

> On average, government interventions reduce by 40 percent the rates of child poverty that would theoretically result from market forces being left to themselves [...]. Governments in the countries with the world's lowest levels of child poverty reduce 'market poverty' by 80 percent or more. Governments in the countries with the world's highest poverty rates reduce 'market poverty' by only 10 percent to 15 percent.
>
> [...] Variation in government policy appears to account for most of the variation in child poverty levels between OECD countries. No OECD country devoting 10 percent or more of GDP to social transfers has a child poverty rate higher than 10 per cent. No country devoting less than 5 percent of GDP to such transfers has a child poverty rate of less than 15 percent.[5]

This is why this work concentrates mainly on studying the social policies of those countries that are the most successful on these matters.

Sustainable development

Sustainable development is another strategy for reducing social inequalities in health. Increasingly, the links between health and sustainable development (either of its three aspects, social, economic, and environmental) are known and documented. The data supporting these links cover many questions — the impacts of atmospheric pollution on respiratory health; urban design that encourages or discourages active transport and physical activity; climate change triggering heat waves and other extreme weather conditions and thus causing increased morbidity and mortality; road building and its consequences on road safety; or the links between housing quality, the built environment, and mental health — and these data are numerous. They show that the principles of sustainable development coincide with those of public health.

---

5. UNICEF *Child Poverty in Rich Countries*. Innocenti Report Card 6. UNICEF Innocenti Research Centre, Florence, 2005, p. 2.

The Public Health Agency of Canada has a sustainable development strategy. It is based on the hypothesis that "[p]ublic health is therefore both a pre-condition to, and an outcome of, sustainable development," and states that "[t]here is growing international consensus that public health and sustainable development are interrelated, long-term objectives that must be addressed in an integrated manner."[6]

Both internationally and locally, socio-economic differences modulate exposure to the health risks associated with non-sustainable development. Thus poor countries are more likely than rich countries to suffer the harmful effects of climate change on health. And within the same country, the poor often live in neighbourhoods that are the least verdant and safe, the most polluted and closest to industrial zones or highways. A study by the British government has shown that the more disadvantaged a neighbourhood, the more it features such harmful conditions as air pollution due to industrial or other activity, a paucity of green spaces, an environment unfriendly to biodiversity, flooding risks, poor quality housing, poor water, an excess of garbage, a high number of road collisions, and proximity to landfill sites.

Applying the principles of sustainable development can contribute a lot to reducing social inequalities in health. Because of the many mechanisms entailed by the strategy of sustainable development, both the Commission on social determinants in health and the recent Marmot report (2010) designate it as an important condition for assuring health equity. This strategy leads to concrete results. When a city in the United Kingdom implemented measures to reduce automobile traffic in poor neighbourhoods, the ratio between the rate of injuries in poor neighbourhoods relative to that in rich neighbourhoods dropped from 3.2 to 2.0 in eight years.

---

6. Public Health Agency of Canada. *Sustainable Development Strategy 2007-2010*, Nov. 2006.

CHAPTER 3

The Example of the Nordic Countries

Even between countries with comparable overall levels of wealth, and thus of human and material resources, international comparisons reveal great disparities between indicators of poverty and health. Some countries have succeeded in reducing poverty and inequalities. Studying the policies and strategies they use to reach this goal is thus of interest. The European Union, in fact, invites its members to compete in striving towards such goals, periodically suggesting action plans against poverty that describe the most promising policies implemented by the most successful countries.

The fight against poverty

Some societies succeed better than others in creating health-promoting environments. Leaders at this are the Nordic countries: Sweden, Norway, Denmark, and Finland. Year after year, they are at the top of the lists ranking countries by indicators of low poverty and equity.

The Human Poverty Index (HPI) developed by the United Nations Development Programme (UNDP) is of particular interest in studies of social inequalities, for it measures social exclusion and life expectancy as well as poverty. The HPI is a composite of the following four indicators: the probability of living a long, healthy life; the percentage of adults able to read and write; the percentage of the population living below the poverty line; and social exclusion, as measured by the long-term unemployment rate.

When developed countries are ranked according to the lowest rates of human poverty by the HPI, the Nordic countries contend for top place (see Table 3.1).

TABLE 3.1

Ranking of the OECD countries by the Human Poverty Index

Ranking 2009		Ranking 2005		Ranking 2000	
1st	Sweden	1st	Sweden	1st	Norway
2nd	Norway	2nd	Norway	2nd	Sweden
3rd	Netherlands	3rd	Netherlands	3rd	Netherlands
4th	Denmark	4th	Finland	4th	Finland
5th	Finland	5th	Denmark	5th	Denmark

Until the mid-2000s, the Nordic countries, with the Czech Republic, France, and Hungary, shared the first five places in the OECD ranking for the lowest rates of economic poverty. The rates of poverty (the proportion of the population with incomes less than 50 percent of the median income for the country) varied from 5 percent to 7 percent. In comparison, the poverty rates for the same period in Canada and the United States were 12 percent and 17 percent, respectively.

In 2010, the four Nordic countries studied ranked among the first six amongst OECD countries for their low percentage of "people who find living on their present income difficult, or very difficult."[1] (The two other countries in the first six places were Luxemburg and the Netherlands.) In 2011 (latest OECD figures available in 2015), Denmark, Finland and Norway ranked third, fourth, and fifth, and Sweden had slipped to the tenth place of 28 OECD countries.

In the domain of child poverty, the Nordic countries post excellent results. At the end of the 2000s, as at the beginning, the four countries studied ranked amongst the first five places, with rates varying from 2 to 4 percent at the beginning of the decade, and from 4 to 7 percent at the end. Canada and Quebec did poorly; both had rates of 15 precent. In 2013, the five Nordic countries were still all classed in the first seven places among the 29 economically advanced countries. The table below shows the percentage of children living in poverty according to figures available in 2014 and compiled by OECD.

As we have seen, poor children are at much greater risk than others of having learning difficulties that reduce their chances of finding decent socio-economic positions — and this, in turn, is linked to health. Therefore

---

1. OECD. *Society at a Glance 2011 - OECD Social Indicators*, 2011.

FIGURE 3.1

Poverty rates for children and the total population. 2010*

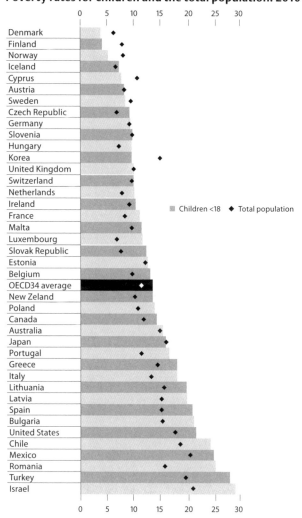

Source: OCDE Family Database, Paris, 2015. www.oecd.org/social/family/database
* Data refer to 2009 for Hungary, Ireland, Japan, New Zealand, Switzerland and Turkey; 2011 for Chile.
Poverty thresholds are set at 50% of the median equivalised disposable income of the entire population.

it is reasonable to claim that, in the long term, fighting child poverty prevents adult poverty.

Reducing inequalities

Income gaps in the Nordic countries are less wide than elsewhere and, when one considers lifestyles, so too are inequalities. The 2005 report of the United Nations Development Programme ranked the OECD countries by income inequality. The Observatoire des inégalités, the French observatory of inequality, summarized the situation in these terms:

> The ratio between the average income of the richest 10 percent and the poorest 10 percent in 2003 was:
> - Six for three Nordic countries, Sweden, Norway, and Finland;
> - Between seven and eight for Denmark, Belgium, and Germany;
> - Nine for the Netherlands, Spain, and France.
> The countries with Anglo-Saxon roots lagged behind, with ratios of 12.5 for Australia, 13.8 for the United Kingdom and, at the bottom of the list, 16 for the United States (UNDP 2005).[2]

In 2011, the OECD published the ranking of its member countries according to the Gini coefficient, a measure of income inequality. The four Nordic countries, along with Slovakia and the Czech Republic, were ranked among the first seven places, with the narrowest income gaps. The two graphics below clearly illustrate the differences, measured by Gini coefficients, between the Nordic countries and other rich countries. It also shows how income gaps have widened everywhere between 1975 and 2008.

In the domain of inequalities between men and women, it is clear that the Nordic countries are the winners here too. Between 1996, when the United Nations index of female participation was first published, and its last edition, in 2009, Sweden, Norway, Denmark, and Finland were always among the five highest ranked countries in the world (except for three years during which one or another of these four countries dropped just below

2. "*Le rapport entre le revenu moyen des 10 % les plus riches et celui des 10 % les plus pauvres est en 2003:*
- *de 6 dans trois pays nordiques: la Suède, la Norvège, la Finlande,*
- *de 7 à 8 en Belgique au Danemark et en Allemagne,*
- *de 9 aux Pays-Bas et en Espagne, comme en France. Les pays du modèle anglo-saxon sont à la traîne: 12,5 en Australie, 13,8 au Royaume-Uni, et, en queue de peloton, 16 aux Etats-Unis.*"
Observatoire des inégalités. Les inégalités ne sont pas une fatalité, 2006. [www.inegalites.fr/spip.php?article590. Accessed on Feb 2, 2014.]

FIGURE 3.2

Income inequality in Nordic countries and other rich countries, based on Gini coefficients

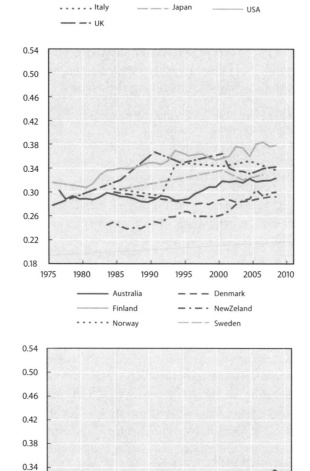

Source: OECD (2011). *Divided We Stand: Why Inequality Keeps Rising*, OECD Publishing, Paris.

fifth place). This index took into account the representation of women in parliament, management, and professional and technical positions, and their salaries relative to those of men.

Decent living conditions

In calling for the health equity gap to be closed within a generation, the Commission on Social Determinants of Health targeted several domains of intervention aimed at improving the population's living conditions. These domains are the following:

- High-quality and accessible education, a high rate of literacy, and a low school dropout rate (Equity from the Start*)
- A major stock of public or subsidized housing (Healthy Places, Healthy People*)
- Generous measures for balancing family and work and for assuring social inclusion via work (Fair Employment and Decent Work*)
- Extended social protection (Social Protection Across the Lifecourse*)
- A high proportion of women working or elected, women's incomes (Gender Equity*)
- High rates of electoral participation, a developed local democracy, and a high degree of press freedom (Political Empowerment – Inclusion and Voice*)
- A relatively extensive redistribution of wealth (Fair Distribution of Power, Money, and Resources*).

Performance measurements in these domains show several Scandinavian countries with rates that are the best, or amongst the best, in the world. The following chapters discuss Nordic policies that encourage success in these domains.

Sustainable development

The Nordic countries have had enviable success in each of the three dimensions of sustainable development: environmental, social, and economic.

In 2005, four Nordic countries were in the first five places as measured by the Environmental Sustainability Index (ESI), developed at Yale and

---

* Titles of chapters or sections of CSDH (2008), *Closing the gap in a generation: health equity through action on the social determinants of health. Final Report of the Commission on Social Determinants of Health* and *Executive Summary,* Geneva, World Health Organization.

Columbia universities in collaboration with the World Economic Forum and the European Commission. Finland was in first place, Norway in second, Sweden in fourth, and Iceland in fifth. Uruguay was in third place, Canada in sixth, Denmark in twenty-sixth, and the United States in forty-fifth.

More recently, the designers have modified the ESI so that it now uses outcome-oriented indicators and is more easily used by decision-makers. The new Environmental Performance Index (EPI) compiles measures of 25 variables in ten categories ranging from air pollution to biodiversity, and including agriculture, climate change, and morbidity attributable to the environment. Table 3.2 shows how the Nordic countries rated in 2008 and 2010 according to this index.

TABLE 3.2

EPI scores of the Nordic countries

In 2008	In 2010
2nd place: Norway	1st place: Iceland
3rd place: Sweden	4th place: Sweden
4th place: Finland	5th place: Norway

Switzerland was in first place in 2008 and in second place in 2010, while Costa Rica was in third place in 2010. It is interesting to note that Canada, in sixth place in 2005, fell to 46th place in 2010.

The Nordic countries have managed, up to now, to preserve healthy environments and effective systems of social protection while also presenting respectable economic performances. According to the World Economic Forum, the Nordic countries' economies are among the most competitive in the world. In 2011, Sweden ranked second in the world, followed by Finland in seventh place and Denmark in ninth (out of 144 countries). In 2014, all four Nordic countries studied were classed in the first thirteen places.

CHAPTER 4

The Characteristics
of the Nordic Countries' Policies

The Nordic model — that is, the modes of governance specific to
Scandinavia and Finland — has been the subject of numerous analyses
over the years. Despite the major reforms and budget cuts the welfare states
went through in the 1990s, the model endures. Even the ways in which
these reforms were orchestrated highlight notable variations between the
Nordic countries and the rest of Europe.

All Nordic policies that in one way or another reduce social inequalities
in health share several common characteristics in how they are developed
and applied. An examination of these characteristics, and of their under-
lying principles, casts an interesting light on the philosophy of Nordic
societies. Such an examination would be incomplete without an overview
of some of their distinctive features which, though not directly concerned
with public policies, allow us to better understand and explain the success
of the Nordic model.

The similarity between the policies of the Nordic countries and the
recommendations of the WHO Commission on Social Determinants of
Health is such that the reader will find that each characteristic described
below is headed by the corresponding Commission's recommendation.

Universality and social protection

"It is important for population health in general, and health of lower soci-
oeconomic groups in particular, that social protection systems are designed
such that they are universal in scope. [...] In other words, social protection

is provided as a social right (Marshall, 1950), rather than given to just the poor out of pity (Lundberg et al., 2007)."[1]

The principle of universality: basic protection for all, without distinction

Access to employment is the preferred way to allow the entire population to participate in a country's social and economic development. The social advantages linked to holding a job offer extended social protection. But though holding a job is highly favoured, universality remains the fundamental principle. The simple fact of living in a Nordic country guarantees very extensive social protection through the following measures: basic old age pensions, disability benefits, social services, health services, guaranteed welfare benefits. These measures apply without regard to a person's current or past work status.

According to Lewis (2001): "The [Scandinavian] model is a universalist one with provision for 'difference' grafted on." She also writes: "The system is based on a commitment to universal citizenship entitlements rather than, as in the United States, on grafting equal citizenship obligations onto a residual welfare model."[2] This universality is made possible by contributions from workers. In exchange, workers benefit from additional social advantages linked to their work, and great flexibility during the course of their professional life. This flexibility allows them to leave work temporarily during various times in their lives and, taking advantage of the generous measures encouraging a balance between work and family responsibilities, to become, say, the natural care giver for a parent or relative. "Sweden comes closest to [the] ideal in that all adult citizens are obliged to engage in paid work in order to qualify for a wide range of benefits, which then permit them to leave the labor market."[3]

---

1. WHO Commission on Social Determinants of Health. *Closing the gap in a generation: Health equity through action on the social determinants of health. Final Report.* World Health Organization, Geneva, 2008, p. 87. [http://whqlibdoc.who.int/publications/2008/9789241563703_eng.pdf?ua=1.]

2. Lewis, J. The decline of the male breadwinner model: implications for work and care. *Social Politics*, vol. 8, no. 2, 2001, p. 163-164.

3. Lewis, J. The decline of the male breadwinner model: implications for work and care. *Social Politics*, vol. 8, no. 2, 2001, p. 163.

Extended admissibility to programs

The extent of admissibility to welfare programs constitutes another characteristic of Nordic policies. The welfare programs support not only the most destitute, but also people who are neither rich nor poor. This is a different perspective from that prevalent in North America, where such programs uniquely target very poor citizens, leaving those who are neither rich nor poor in a precarious situation.

The perspective of the Nordic countries ensures that middle-class citizens also benefit from welfare programs and social protection. Aware of the role and the significant advantages of these programs, such citizens are more inclined to contribute fiscally to these measures, thus assuring the sustainability of the distribution of wealth.

Awareness of the role of social protection could be associated with the people's perception of the causes of social inequalities. A Canadian study compared the proportions of people in Canada, Norway, and the United States who believe that social inequalities are due to laziness. The proportion of people who believe that laziness is the root of social inequalities is less in countries with significant protection measures. For example, 10.8 percent of Norwegians believe that social inequalities are due to laziness. This percentage rises to 31 percent in Canada and to 37.5 percent in the United States.

Prevention first and foremost

"Social protection schemes can be instrumental in realizing developmental goals, rather than being dependent on achieving these goals — they can be efficient ways to reduce poverty, and local economies can benefit."[4]

Social protection policies act preventively. They stop people falling into poverty rather than intervening *a posteriori* in attempts to extricate people from poverty and counter its harmful effects.

Early intervention is a goal both of universal social protection programs and of welfare programs targeted at a substantial portion of the population. In the Nordic countries, social inclusion of citizens of adult age is seen as the result of social investments made during childhood and adolescence.

---

4. WHO Commission on Social Determinants of Health. *Closing the gap in a generation: Health equity through action on the social determinants of health. Final Report.* World Health Organization, Geneva, 2008, p. 7.

Some researchers have set out to verify the efficacy of preventive measures. The aim of a longitudinal study published in 2003 was to assess whether Swedish measures of social protection had succeeded in attenuating the impact of neighbourhood poverty in adolescence on social exclusion in adulthood. In general, neighbourhood characteristics affect a child's future no matter what the family's income. The potential impact of place of residence on several indicators of social exclusion in adulthood, notably educational level and job status, was measured by sampling 15,000 persons over a period of 30 years. The results show that for adults who grew up in poor neighbourhoods, the probabilities of social exclusion were no greater than for their contemporaries who grew up in well-to-do neighbourhoods. According to the authors of the study, it is well established that the income gap varies in width with the type of welfare state. It is, therefore, reasonable to expect that the range of the neighbourhood effect would vary similarly: the more effective the social protection, the less deleterious the neighbourhood effect.

Another study looked at the effect of childhood neighbourhood by measuring a different variable. The salaries of brothers living in the United States were compared to the salaries of brothers living in the Nordic countries. The results: the correlation between brothers' salaries was much stronger in the United States than in the Nordic countries. Since most brothers grow up in the same neighbourhood, these results suggest that both the effects of the neighbourhood in which adolescents live and the effects of their family are greater in the United States than in the Nordic countries. It also suggests that social policies that attenuate such neighbourhood and family effects have a stronger foothold, or are more effective, in the Nordic countries.

Policy integration

"An overarching Commission recommendation is the need for intersectoral coherence — in policy-making and action — to enhance effective action on the social determinants of health and achieve improvements in health equity."[5]

The Nordic social policies are designed so as to coordinate the missions of various ministries and government agencies in various sectors of state intervention and economic activity. Moreover, they contribute to reaching all of the state's diverse goals.

---

5. WHO Commission on Social Determinants of Health. *Closing the gap in a generation: Health equity through action on the social determinants of health. Final Report.* World Health Organization, Geneva, 2008, p. 22.

The integrated approach

The integrated approach, which characterizes the design and implementation of policies, aims at guiding the actions of all ministries and government agencies. The goal is to increase the coherence of programs and ensure that citizens are better served.

Gender-equity policies and those for handicapped persons illustrate this approach well. They must apply in all ministries and agencies (horizontal application), and be reflected in the actions of both ministers and civil servants (vertical application). This is why, in Sweden, courses on male-female equity are designed for an intended audience of ministers, political advisers, press attachés, and civil servants. In the same spirit, state employees are trained about handicaps so that they can help handicapped persons exercise their rights as citizens and avoid putting them into humiliating circumstances simply because of ignorance of their situations.

The importance of complementarity and multisectorality

Whether they deal with, for example, the job market, housing, or last-resort financial assistance, social policies have complementary goals. This is why it is deemed necessary to intervene in each sector rather than to limit policies with social effect only to some sectors.

The social inclusion of parents and children of single-parent families is a positive and convincing example of this. Such inclusion is simultaneously facilitated by work standards, which offer great flexibility in work hours in the years after the birth of a child; by a system of universal and free education of high quality; and by an alimony paid by the State in cases in which a parent who does not have custody fails to meet his or her obligations, or cannot do so. Sweden pioneered such living allowances for single mothers in 1917.

The redistribution of wealth

"The generosity of social protection systems – Health and health equity are influenced not just by the degree of universalism, but also by the degree of generosity of social protection policies (Lundberg et al., 2007)."[6]

---

6. WHO Commission on Social Determinants of Health. *Closing the gap in a generation: Health equity through action on the social determinants of health. Final Report.* World Health Organization, Geneva, 2008, p. 90.

FIGURE 4.1

Social transfers relating to family and other issues as percentage of GDP

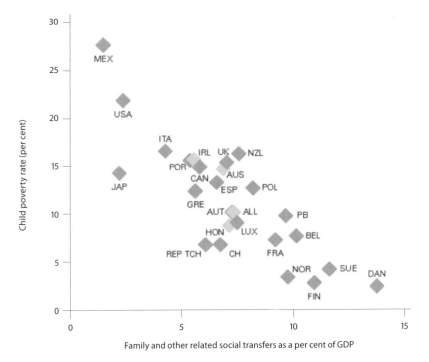

Source: UNICEF. *Child Poverty in Rich Countries*, Innocenti Research Centre, Florence, 2005, p. 23.

As we saw in the preceding chapter, income gaps are narrower in the Nordic countries than elsewhere in the world, and disparities between life-styles are less. The Gini coefficient is a measure of level of inequality. A score of 0 signifies perfect equality, while a score of 1 indicates extreme inequality (that is, the hypothetical case in which one person owns all a collectivity's wealth). The average Gini score for family income in the Scandinavian countries is .26. For the European Union it is .30; for Canada, .32; and for the United States, 39. The rates of poverty in Scandinavia, as measured by the United Nations Development Programme's Human Poverty Index, are also among the lowest of the developed countries.

As a corollary, public expenditures, especially social expenditures, are high in the Nordic countries. Since their effect is to redistribute wealth, they represent a major fraction of the gross domestic product (GDP). In

2014, Sweden invested 28 percent of its GDP in public social expenses (retirement pension plans, income support, health, etc.), while Denmark invested 30 percent, Finland 31 percent, and Norway 22 percent. In that same year such expenditures accounted for an average of 22 percent of GDP in OECD countries, and for 17 percent in Canada.

In its report *Child poverty in rich countries*, UNICEF shows that there is a correlation between the fraction of public expenditures on social and familial benefits, and the rate of child poverty: the larger the fraction of its GDP a government invests in such benefits, the lower the rate of child poverty. Figure 4.1 compares the OECD countries and clearly shows the links between social transfers and rates of child poverty.

Gender equity as a fundamental principle of public policy

"Gender mainstreaming – The Commission recommends that: Governments and international institutions set up within the central administration and provide adequate and long-term funding for a gender equity unit that is mandated to analyse and to act on the gender equity implications of policies, programmes, and institutional arrangements."[7]

Gender equity is a fundamental principle in policy design, and one of the predominant characteristics of the Nordic countries. Not only social policies, but all public policies are absolutely required to integrate this perspective. According the Jørgenson, "gender equity may be considered one of the pillars of the Scandinavian welfare states."[8] Brachet, another researcher, confirms this: "There is general agreement that the policy of gender equity should apply in all domains of life. Politically this theme has become particularly dominant in employment and family policies."[9]

The policies of equity establish goals which all ministries and governmental agencies must take into account in designing and implementing

7. WHO Commission on Social Determinants of Health. *Closing the gap in a generation: Health equity through action on the social determinants of health. Final Report.* World Health Organization, Geneva, 2008, p. 148.

8. *"[L]'égalité des sexes peut être considérée comme l'un des piliers des États providence scandinaves."* Jørgensen, H. Le rôle des syndicats dans les réformes sociales en Scandinavie dans les années quatre-vingt-dix. *Revue française des affaires sociales*, vol. 4, n° 4, 2003, p. 129.

9. *"La politique de l'égalité des sexes est devenue l'objet d'un large consensus devant s'appliquer à tous les domaines de la vie. En politique, ce thème est particulièrement dominant dans la politique de l'emploi et dans la politique familiale."* Brachet, S. *Politique familiale et assurance parentale en Suède: une synthèse*, Dossiers d'étude - Allocations familiales, CNAF (Caisse nationale d'allocations familiales), Paris, 2001, p. 19.

their own policies. 'Gender mainstreaming' is the term used to designate this dominant concept. A report on social inclusion by Denmark's Ministry of Social Affairs and its Ministry of Interior Affairs and Health refers to it in these words: "The Danish Gender Equality Act provides that public authorities must within their respective areas of responsibility seek to promote equal opportunities and incorporate gender equality in all planning and administration. To fulfill this obligation, comprehensive cross-ministerial work has been ongoing for several years, the aim being to create new tools and methods for gender equality."[10]

It is the state's responsibility to train the ministries and verify that these objectives are integrated. In Denmark, each new law is examined to determine if it needs to be submitted to thorough evaluation from the point of view of gender equity. In Sweden, all ministries are required to present propositions relative to this question in their fields of responsibility. Moreover, several government entities dedicated to gender equity have been created. These include the Division for Gender Equality, responsible for supporting the ministries in integrating the gender equality perspective in all policies.

Equal opportunity, financial autonomy, the desexualization of roles in private and public life, and power and influence, both individual and collective are the favoured routes to equity. The actual means of achieving equity resides in the rigorous application of the various policies that have been refined by sophisticated systems of evaluation.

High employment rate and measures for supporting employment

"To date, relatively few countries have integrated employment and working conditions into economic and social policies. To make this happen means redressing the power balance between private and public actors."[11]

Active labour-market policies — policies that encourage the population to contribute to the productivity of society, that is, that encourage activation — are also among the pillars of the Nordic model. Like the policies of gender equity, they have transverse goals and apply in several domains. At the heart of strategies of gender equity, social inclusion, social protec-

---

10. Denmark. Ministry of Social Affairs, Ministry of Interior Affairs and Health. *National Report on Strategies for Social Protection and Social Inclusion*. 2006, p. 6.
11. WHO Commission on Social Determinants of Health. *Closing the gap in a generation: Health equity through action on the social determinants of health. Final Report.* World Health Organization, Geneva, 2008, p. 77.

tion, and economic policies are a number of measures that maximize the number of people who hold jobs.

"Full and fair employment and decent work be made a shared objective of international institutions and a central part of national policy agendas and development strategies"[12]

The policies take into account that activation results not only from holding a job, but from exercising various functions in private life — such as educating a child or caring for a family member who has lost autonomy — that contribute to the productivity of society. This vision of activation explains, among other things, the generous measures for balancing work and family.

Like liberal regimes elsewhere, the welfare systems of the Nordic countries stress activation of the greatest numbers, but with the difference that, in these countries, public measures that help people hold jobs, as well as working conditions, are markedly better. The policies also accord great importance to continuing training to help those who have lost a job find new work, and to maintain a high level of competitiveness in the workforce.

The Nordic governments consider the offer of such generous activation programs to their citizens to be an investment worth its weight in gold. First, the investment serves to fight poverty by ensuring access to incomes. Second, it gives people power over their lives. When people, particularly immigrants, acquire autonomy and economic independence (by means of employment programs for the handicapped, for instance) they can fully participate in the life of society. Third, the investment empowers people, giving them the opportunity to realize their potential and contribute to the life of their community. As well, the investment earns money. The emphasis that governments put on activation measures means they collect substantial taxes, thus increasing the pool of financial resources needed for social protection and numerous social investments.

The lifecourse approach

"All people need social protection across the lifecourse, as young children, in working life, and in old age. People also need protection in case of specific shocks, such as illness, disability, and loss of income or work."[13]

---

12. Ibid., p. 202.
13. WHO Commission on Social Determinants of Health. *Closing the gap in a generation: Health equity through action on the social determinants of health. Final Report.* World Health Organization, Geneva, 2008, p. 7.

More systematically and explicitly than elsewhere, the policies of the Nordic countries integrate principles that take account of the lifecourse of citizens and the multidimensional reality of life. In other words, a worker is not just a worker but also a son, parent, partner or, possibly, caregiver. The policies described above — social protection and prevention, policy integration, redistribution of wealth, gender equity, and activation — correspond to the principles of the lifecourse approach. This approach aims to take into account as much as possible the various dimensions of life and complexity of a person's lifecourse, and their long-term repercussions.

According to Bernard and his collaborators (2006), the lifecourse approach is based on four principles that public policies should take into account:

1.   A lifecourse takes shape in time. This principle implies that today's choices have consequences on tomorrow's reality. For example, the choice of staying at home to raise young children has repercussions on the amounts that accumulate in a person's pension plan.

2.   Life consists of multiple, intertwined facts. "Individuals engage in constant exchanges with numerous institutions (…) such as the family, the community, the market, and the state. Resources are transferred between individuals and various institutions. These include income (…), education, literacy, and social relations."[14] According to this principle, all these resources are interlinked with the policies that strongly affect how they are distributed.

3.   Lifecourses are interlinked. This principle refers, for example, to the fact that one person's lack of a job may affect his or her entire family. "Child poverty follows from parental poverty and thus involves not only solutions aimed at children (daycares, for instance) but also at parents (such as measures of social aid and family support)."[15]

---

14. "*Les individus entretiennent des échanges constants avec de nombreuses institutions (…) comme la famille, la communauté, le marché et l'État. Des ressources sont transférées entre les individus et les différentes institutions qui incluent le revenu (…), l'éducation et la littératie, les relations sociales.*" Bernard, P. *La perspective des parcours de vie*, Appendix to the program Inégalités sociales et marché du travail, Université de Montréal, Sociology Department, 2007, p. 9.

15. "*La pauvreté infantile découle de la pauvreté des parents et, donc, implique des solutions visant les enfants (les garderies, par exemple), mais aussi les parents (mesures d'aide sociale, de soutien aux familles).*" Ibid.

4. Lifecourses unfold in socially constructed milieus. This principle assumes that the culture of the society in which one grows up and the political system in which one lives have multiple repercussions. "Thus, the lifecourses of those living in a specific place are affected by local and regional contexts and by social and historical contexts (…), particularly in the case of persons with limited ability to travel (children, the aged, the handicapped, and the poor)."[16]

This approach dictates a long-term perspective, one in which "differences between even limited initial possibilities tend to be amplified over time."[17] Moreover, the study of social inequalities in health convincingly illustrates the fact that health status at a given moment is determined by, among other things, the accumulated effects of prior life circumstances, including quite early ones. The approach agrees with the principle of prevention so dear to the Nordic countries. In effect, their policies recognize that social investments made during childhood and adolescence can lead to social inclusion during adulthood.

A tradition of consensus

"Fair representation of workers in developing the national policy agenda: public sector leadership is critical, nationally and globally, and requires mechanisms that strengthen the representation of all workers and those seeking work in the creation of policy, legislation, and programmes relating to employment and work."[18]

The search for consensus is a determining element in the state's relations with unions, businesses, citizens' groups, and other partners. Consensus decision-making is not only widespread amongst the governments of the Nordic countries, but is also a practice rooted in tradition. There has even been talk of a cult of consensus. "Network governance in terms of coordinating a mix of civil servants, politicians, academics, experts,

---

16. "*Contextes locaux et régionaux, contextes sociétaux et contextes historiques (…) ont donc un effet sur les trajectoires de vie des personnes qui y résident, particulièrement dans le cas des personnes dont les possibilités de déplacement sont limitées (enfants, personnes âgées, personnes handicapées, personnes pauvres).*" Ibid.
17. "*Les différences dans les possibilités initiales, même limitées, tendent à être amplifiées au fil du temps.*" Ibid.
18. WHO Commission on Social Determinants of Health. *Closing the gap in a generation: Health equity through action on the social determinants of health. Final Report.* World Health Organization, Geneva, 2008, p. 77.

and representatives of relevant civil society organisations is to a large extent a rather institutionalised mode of making public policy in Sweden."[19]

Several examples support this claim. When the Finnish and Swedish pension schemes were reformed in the late 1990s, the basic principles were formulated at the beginning of the reform process by the state's partners (unions and employers). There are similar examples in the community sector. For instance, in the Swedish policy on services for handicapped persons, the definition of personal assistance is almost identical to the definition of the ideal such service drawn up by the Independent Living Institute. One of the most important organizations lobbying for rights for the handicapped in Sweden, this institute pioneered the very idea of personal assistance, and is a leader in the independent living movement. In designing its policies, the government has always consulted handicapped persons' groups. It even created a commission to serve as a forum for exchanges between the state and these groups.

Similarly, the mechanisms by which salary levels are fixed — there is no statutory minimum wage — illustrate the 'cult' of consensus. In the Nordic countries, traditionally, salary scales were decided by consensus after a process of tripartite negotiations between employers, unions, and local or national governments. The high rates of unionization facilitate this kind of process. It should be noted, however, that union policies "allow the national economy to be competitive, balanced, and fair, all at the same time. This implies that macroeconomic and sectoral politics are coordinated. It also implies that social partners are inclined to enter into salary negotiations in a way that takes into account both productivity gains and salary increases in other countries."[20] Unfortunately, there has been a decline in recent years of this mode of central negotiation in some work areas.

19. Hall, P. and S. Montin. *Governance Networks and Democracy at Regional and Local Level in Sweden*. Roskilde: Roskilde University, Centre for democratic network governance. Working Paper 2007:9, p.1.
20. *"Permettent à l'économie nationale d'être à la fois compétitive, équilibrée et juste. Ceci suppose de coordonner les politiques macroéconomiques et les politiques sectorielles. Ceci suppose également que les partenaires sociaux soient enclins à aborder les négociations salariales d'une manière qui tienne compte à la fois des gains de productivité et de la hausse des salaires dans les autres pays."* Jørgensen, H. Le rôle des syndicats dans les réformes sociales en Scandinavie dans les années quatre-vingt-dix. *Revue française des affaires sociales*, vol. 4, n° 4, 2003, p. 128. [Our translation.]

Democracy and power at the local level

"While the empowerment of social groups through their representation in policy-related agenda-setting and decision-making is critical, so too is empowerment for action through bottom-up, grassroots approaches (Sibal, 2006). The struggles against the injustices encountered by the most disadvantaged in society, and the process of organizing these people, builds local people's leadership. It is empowering. It gives people a greater sense of control over their lives and future."[21]

In Sweden, Norway, Denmark, and Finland, government power is decentralized in numerous domains — in health, social services, education, daycare, and other services that help assure social protection and inclusion. Municipal and regional authorities, in other words, are responsible for managing and providing these services. It may be of interest to note that there are now 290 municipal governments in Sweden, whereas twenty years ago there were more than two thousand. National financial resources are allocated at levels determined to be appropriate by the evaluation of local needs. Municipalities also have significant taxing powers, which assure their capacity to pay for all services.

The Nordic countries have in common another form of power sharing: the entities responsible for designing programs are distinct from those responsible for implementation. Thus, ministries design programs which government agencies (of which there are three hundred in Sweden) independently implement. The ministries, which have relatively few employees, set priorities, define policies, set basic goals, and transfer money to government agencies. The latter have the power to make intermediate decisions. They also evaluate the effects of policies on the ground. Auger (1998) put it well: "Instead of delivering services itself, the state is concerned with goals and results. The daily activities and the actual delivery of goods and services are the responsibility of organizations that are close to the citizen."[22]

---

21. WHO Commission on Social Determinants of Health. *Closing the gap in a generation: Health equity through action on the social determinants of health. Final Report.* World Health Organization, Geneva, 2008, p. 162.

22. "*L'État se préoccupe des objectifs et des résultats au lieu de produire lui-même les services. Les activités quotidiennes et la production des biens et services sont sous la responsabilité d'organismes près du citoyen.*" Auger, J. Réforme de l'administration publique: Suède. *Coup d'œil*, vol. 4, no. 2, 1998, p. 7.

Decentralization also implies interaction with citizens' groups in democratic processes. Here is a description of the position of the Scandinavian unions, which participate actively and significantly in the political and administrative systems:

> The Scandinavian countries are small, decentralized countries in which municipalities are responsible for supplying most social services and benefits, and do so in the context of strong democratic traditions. The municipalities hold strategic positions in the politico-administrative system, make the majority of public expenditures, take care of most assistance services, and are close to citizens. Proximity to citizens is indispensable for democracy in all domains of public policy.[23]

In Sweden, for example, almost all municipalities have consultative committees that collaborate systematically with citizen interest groups, such as groups of the retired or of the handicapped. Citizen involvement and feedback inform the process of making political decisions. This type of network governance was introduced in Sweden at the beginning of the 1970s.

Science and social and health research

"Measure the problem, evaluate action, expand the knowledge base, develop a workforce that is trained in the social determinants of health, and raise public awareness about the social determinants of health."[24]

Addressing the 1969 congress of the Swedish Social Democratic Party, during a discussion of the scientific nature of the decision-making process, Olof Palme, former Prime Minister of Sweden, said: "Rather than a social democracy, I prefer to call our society a 'study-circle democracy.'"[25]

---

23. *"Les pays scandinaves sont de petits pays décentralisés dans lesquels les municipalités sont responsables de fournir la plupart des services et prestations sociales et le font dans le cadre de fortes traditions démocratiques. Les municipalités occupent des positions stratégiques dans le système politico-administratif, elles engagent la majorité des dépenses publiques, assument la plupart des missions d'assistance et sont proches des citoyens. La proximité est une condition indispensable à la démocratie, qui devrait s'appliquer à tous les domaines des politiques publiques."* Jørgensen, H. Le rôle des syndicats dans les réformes sociales en Scandinavie dans les années quatre-vingt-dix. *Revue française des affaires sociales*, vol. 4, no. 4, 2003, p. 128.
24. WHO Commission on Social Determinants of Health. *Closing the gap in a generation: Health equity through action on the social determinants of health. Final Report.* World Health Organization, Geneva, 2008, p. 2.
25. Cited in Milner, H. *Civic Literacy: How Informed Citizens Make Democracy Work.* University Press of New England, Hanover, 2002, p. 105.

The Nordic countries have a long tradition of social and health research. It is part of their political culture to make evaluations systematically so that political decisions are, usually, based on hard evidence. Many examples support this claim.

After a major recession hit Sweden in the 1990s, the government, in collaboration with the Nordic Council of Ministers, commissioned a study to assess the state of social protection for citizens during this decade. The central goal of the study was to produce an exhaustive evaluation to serve as a base for future policy directions.

At the local level, the city of Helsinki, which has responsibility for managing primary and secondary schools, requires that its schools produce, each year, a global evaluation of their accomplishments. The aim is to improve learning conditions and support the development of teaching. The evaluation practices are based on a strategy presented by the city in a document entitled *Evaluation Strategy of General Teaching*. The prime foci of this strategy are academic results, the transmission of learning skills, and health and other services in the school.

Recently the Swedish government wanted to verify whether, ten years after its promulgation, the law prohibiting the sale of sexual services had had its intended results. Studies led to publication in 2011 of a report that estimated street prostitution had dropped by 50 percent. (To learn more about this law and its effects, see the chapter on gender equity.)

In 2008 the Swedish government asked the University of Gothenburg to produce hard data on what employees of government agencies should do to better apply the integrated approach in dealing with gender equity issues. This was not a question of evaluating the consequences of an intervention, but rather of supporting and equipping the interveners.

Moreover, the results of scientific research are often included in public documents. Thus there is a partiality for communicating the data on which policies are based so as to educate the population and share knowledge. On the website of the Norwegian Ministry of Health, for instance, one can read a document that explains the links between health and income in Norway and shows mortality rates by income bracket. This document describes the steady widening of income inequalities during recent years, explains how the Gini coefficient measures income inequality and discusses its limits, and gives Gini scores for various countries.

The Swedish government, too, makes scientific information accessible. According to Raphael et al.: "The Swedish health authorities show remarkable skill in taking the latest data on the determinants of health and transmitting them in comprehensible form to the general public."[26]

Unionization and the contribution of unions

"Unions are powerful vehicles through which protection for workers — nationally and internationally — can be collectively negotiated."[27]

A large fraction of the population of the countries under study is unionized. In 2014, 67 percent of wage-earners in Denmark were unionized, compared to 71 percent in Sweden, 74 percent in Finland and 52 percent in Norway. In comparison, in 2012 the rate of unionization was 40 percent in Quebec and 32 percent in Canada. In the United States the rate dropped from 20 percent in 1983 to 11 percent in 2014.

Despite the high rates of unionization, the number of strikes is rather low. This can be explained by the fact that negotiations are often tripartite — state or local community, union, and employer — and are conducted in a spirit of conciliation.

The unions contribute to the definition of policy orientation, as they did at the end of the 1990s, at the time of the reforms of social and employment policies following the recession of Northern Europe at the beginning of that decade. These reforms were made in response to the imperatives of market globalization. Nevertheless, they kept social protection as an essential element of the model, relying on collective engagement and the willingness to invest in, and pay for, the costs of maintaining high standards.

Multipartite governments and the proportional voting system

"Any serious effort to reduce health inequities will involve changing the distribution of power within society…"[28]

The parliamentary systems of Denmark, Sweden, Norway, and Finland welcome representatives of several political parties, each of which is repre-

26. Raphael, D., T. Bryant, and M. Rioux (eds.). *Staying Alive: Critical Perspectives on Health, Illness, and Health Care*, 2nd edition, Canadian Scholars' Press, Toronto, 2006, p. 422.

27. WHO Commission on Social Determinants of Health. *Closing the gap in a generation: Health equity through action on the social determinants of health. Final Report.* World Health Organization, Geneva, 2008, p. 77.

28. WHO Commission on Social Determinants of Health. *Closing the gap in a generation: Health equity through action on the social determinants of health. Final Report.* World Health Organization, Geneva, 2008, p. 18.

sented as a function of the number of votes obtained. The proportional representation method allows parties to sit in Parliament as soon as they obtain, nation-wide, either four percent of the votes (in Sweden and Norway), or two percent (in Denmark).

Coalition governments are very common in Denmark. In fact, since no government has had a majority since 1909, public policies are characterized by compromise among the parties. Considering that compromise is also the method by which salary minima are fixed — for example by agreement between public service unions and the government — it's clear that multipartite agreements really are the way Danes do politics.

The proportional representation system encourages representation of the greatest diversity of perspectives and minority points of view, thus increasing citizens' political power. It also encourages the election of women, thus increasing gender equity. The proportions of women members of parliament in the Nordic countries — 45 percent in Sweden, 43 percent in Finland, 40 percent in Norway, and 39 percent in Denmark — are among the highest in the world. By comparison, after the most recent elections in the United States, 19 percent of the seats in congress are held by women. In Canada, women account for 25 percent of MPs and 27 percent of MNAs in Quebec.

From the historical point of view, one of the main reasons Sweden has avant-garde social policies is that it has been governed by a series of social-democratic governments. The Social Democratic Party was in power from 1930 to 2006, with the exception of nine years (from 1976 to 1982, and from 1991 to 1994). The party gained power thanks to proportional representation; the implementation of this system in 1909 allowed the election, in 1911, of the first leftist parliamentarians.

Finally, the rate of electoral participation is higher in the countries that have adopted the proportional representation method since, by opening the door to several parties, it offers more choice to electors and gives more power to citizens. The electoral participation rates in the Nordic countries are among the best in the world. At the most recent national elections, rates were 88 percent in Denmark in 2007, 86 percent in Sweden in 2014, 78 percent in Norway in 2013, and 67 percent in Finland in 2011.

The governments of these countries recognize the links between citizen participation and equality of opportunity, as shown by Sweden's public health policy, which stresses the link between citizen empowerment and health:

The power and possibility of people to influence the world around them is probably of crucial significance for their health. Societies with a low election turnout, where few people feel there is any point in participating in NGO activities or trying to influence development, are also characterized by the occurrence of serious health problems. Increasing people's level of participation in society is therefore one of the most important national public health objectives.[29]

29. Raphael, D., T. Bryant, and M. Rioux (eds.). *Staying Alive: Critical Perspectives on Health, Illness, and Health Care,* (2nd edition) Canadian Scholars' Press, Toronto, 2006, p. 424.

CHAPTER 5

Family and Work-Life Balancing Policies

The family policies of the Nordic countries emphasize financial support measures, allocation of parental leave, and work-life balance. The three cornerstones of Swedish family policy are family allowances, maternity or paternity leave, and subsidized public daycare. What distinguishes the family policies of the Nordic countries is the breadth and flexibility of their measures.

Policy foundations

In the Nordic countries, parents are not the only ones with responsibility for caring for and educating children; the State must play its part too, in a spirit of "collective solidarity in accepting parental responsibilities."[1] Consequently, several measures support parents while granting them a maximum number of choices.

Measures of financial aid such as universal family benefits, and measures helping to balance family life and work such as parental leave, aim to reinforce parents' power over their own lives and to increase families' freedom of choice. The foundations of family policies are equality between men and women, and balance between professional and family life. The right to work and full employment, characteristics of the Nordic model, also find their place in these policies. They are applied in a perspective of gender equity, for the policies rest on the dual-earner model, in which the man and the woman share family responsibilities.

---

1. "[S]*olidarité collective face aux responsabilités parentales*", Brachet, S. *Politique familiale et assurance parentale en Suède: une synthèse.* Dossiers d'étude - Allocations familiales, CNAF (Caisse nationale d'allocations familiales), Paris, 2001, p. 17.

Credit: Stina Gullander/imagebank.sweden.se

Parental leave in Sweden lasts 480 days, whether a child is adopted or not.

The Swedish state promotes both equality between men and women and the welfare of children. For example, the state actively promotes its program of paternity leave so as to increase the number of participating men. A very widely distributed government brochure clearly summarizes the reasons why a father should take such leave, as indicated in this passage:

> The child has just as much need of his or her father as of the mother. The strongest bonds between parent and child form when the child is still very young. The period during which these bonds form cannot be recaptured later. For the child, an absent father quickly becomes a secondary figure. Looking after a child boosts the ability to socialize and relate. Confronting and solving the problems of daily life with a child will encourage the development of new skills. And being on parental leave develops paternal feelings.[2]

---

2. "*L'enfant a besoin de son père autant que de sa mère. Les liens les plus profonds entre le parent et l'enfant se tissent lorsque l'enfant est encore tout petit. La période où se nouent ces liens est irrécupérable ultérieurement. Un père absent devient vite une figure secondaire pour l'enfant. S'occuper d'un enfant augmente les capacités sociales et relationnelles. Affronter et résoudre des problèmes de la vie quotidienne avec un enfant feront apparaître de nouvelles compétences. Être en congé parental développe le sentiment paternel.*" Brachet, S. *Le congé parental en Suède: implications pour la garde d'enfants de moins de trois ans*, Paris, Institut national d'études démographiques, 2002, p. 56.

The attribution of means-tested benefits — that is, the attribution of benefits such as housing allowances to those whose financial resources are below a certain threshold — is also considered an essential measure contributing to families' freedom of action.

Officially, the policies do not have pro-birth goals, but rather belong to the larger set of interventions typical of states that seek social equity, equal opportunity for all children, and gender equity. It should be noted that the fertility rates in the four countries under study are relatively high: they vary from 1.73 to 1.91. Though these rates are higher than Canada's (1.66) and the average rate of OECD countries (1.74), they (like the rates in almost all Western countries) fall below the threshold replacement fertility rate of 2.1, the rate needed to assure a new generation as populous as the old.

Range and flexibility of measures

Work standards and parental leave benefits make it possible to gauge the range and flexibility of the family policy measures in place. Here are some examples:

- In Sweden, parents are entitled to 60 days leave per year when a child under the age of twelve is sick. As well, they may reduce their work hours by 25 percent without compensation until a child reaches the age of eight. Moreover, parental-training programs are offered by centres of maternal protection. Parents are paid for taking this training.
- The labour law in Norway and the collective agreements implemented in Sweden allow mothers to take breaks to breastfeed their children. In Norway, mothers are entitled to two unpaid half-hours per day for as long as they continue to breastfeed. They are also able to begin their workday an hour later or end it an hour earlier. As for employees of the national and municipal governments, their breastfeeding pauses and free hour are paid, and part-time employees are entitled to the same measures.
- Norwegians can choose between 47 weeks of parental leave and 100 percent of parental benefits, or 57 weeks of leave and 80 percent of these benefits. Like workers, those collecting employment insurance are also eligible for these benefits. Self-employed and freelance workers are also eligible; their benefits are calculated based on their income over the three years preceding the birth of the child.
- As for Swedes, they get sixteen months of parental leave, which they can take in portions at any time until the child reaches eight years of

age. They can also extend their sixteen months by dividing days off work into half-days off. The parental allowance itself can be paid either continuously or discontinuously. Continuous full-time paid leave lasts for sixteen months. Frequently parents take a reduced allowance so as to prolong their leave; for instance, they take half-time paid leave for thirty-two months. The benefit-receiving parent can thus be on full-time leave while receiving a half-time parental allowance. Of course, the parent may also be on leave while working part-time. As well, parents may alternate periods of leave and of work. While on leave, a beneficiary receives 80 percent of his or her salary for the first thirteen months and approximately twenty-eight dollars per day during the remaining three months. Each of the two parents has the right to take half of the days of leave. Alternatively, they may both, at the same time, claim the half-time entitlement. However, two months of the total leave period are reserved exclusively for each parent, and are lost if not utilized; they cannot be transferred.

According to a researcher who has compared the Swedish and French parental leave systems, the great flexibility of the Swedish system allows parents to develop real strategies, determining the ratio between level of allowance and duration of leave, that is, according to their particular financial capabilities and educational preferences, the most suitable.

Policy evaluation

The fight against poverty

Recently, the OECD called attention to the fact that the family policies of the Nordic countries succeed better than those of other OECD countries in preventing child poverty in single-parent families in which the one parent works. Denmark, Norway, and Sweden are the only OECD countries (with the exception of Portugal) in which the children of such families are not poorer than those living in two-parent families in which one of the parents works; but in Portugal, the rates of childhood poverty in single-parent and two-parent families are 26 percent and 33 percent respectively.

Sweden employs several strategies to combat poverty in single-parent families. Few of these measures directly target such families. Rather, in the spirit of universality that characterizes the Nordic countries' policies, the same measures to combat poverty apply to all families, single-parent and two-parent alike.

Rates of childhood poverty in the Nordic countries for all kinds of families combined were between four and eight percent in 2010, among the lowest in the world. In Sweden, similar results are due to the following measures:

- Treatment of quasi-poor families in the same way as poor families. The public authorities remain prudent in assessing the sources of income of families just above the poverty line; such families do not have to depend on the market, for the state continues to transfer benefits, helping them stay out of poverty.
- The measures for balancing home and work duties described above, and high-quality public daycare services. By offering great flexibility to those returning to the job market, these measures allow a large number of mothers to work.
- Guaranteed alimony for separated families. This measure is described below.
- Family and housing benefits. Housing benefits complement the support for single-parent families.
- Prevention of poverty by providing, through transfers from the state, an important fraction of family income. In Sweden the labour market supplies 70 percent of the income of two-parent families, while in Canada this percentage is 85 percent. Despite the difficulties they encounter here in Canada, single-parent families must find 50 percent of their income on the job market. In Sweden, this percentage is about 40 perecent.

Balancing family and work

The aim of measures for balancing family and work duties is to encourage mothers to work, which is one of the best ways of reducing childhood poverty and contributing to gender equity. In Norway, 77.3 percent of women in the active population had jobs in 2010. For men, the proportion was 82.6 percent. This employment rate for women was the second highest in the world. It was topped by Iceland (81.7%), and followed by Denmark (77.2%) and Sweden (77.1%). Despite the fact that many women work, birth rates in these countries are higher than the European average. Moreover, in Norway the female-to-male earnings ratio is, at 1.0, the highest in the world.

In the European countries, interestingly, about 33 percent of women work in the public sector, whereas in the Nordic countries this proportion rises to between 54 and 62 percent.

Credit: Martin Svalander/imagebank.sweden.se

In 2009, fathers in Sweden took 22 percent of the 480 days allowed for parental leave, equivalent to an average of three months of leave.

According to the Swedish Institute, subsidized public daycare, subsidized public centres for the aged, and an improved transport system are among the important factors explaining the high proportion of Swedish women who work. The burden of care giving, which in most countries falls on women, is thus reduced, and it becomes much easier to meet all family and professional obligations.

A study conducted by the European Union and published in 2010 grouped the countries of the Union by similarity of their home-work balancing systems. The group that performed best in terms of the conditions offered was that of the Nordic countries, Denmark, Finland, and Sweden. (Norway is not a member of the EU.) The study concluded that these countries are distinguished by their particularly well-developed daycare services, the ability to return to work after an absence for family reasons, very flexible work hours, and the possibilities of working part-time.

Another study, from the Center for Economic and Policy Research, compared the quality of the parental leave systems in twenty-one rich countries. When these countries were ranked from best to worst, the four countries at the top of the list were Sweden, Norway, Finland, and Greece. The researchers identified five factors of success: the generosity of the remuneration paid during the leave; the large number of weeks of non-transferable leave from one parent to the other, and thus a significant non-transferable period of paternity leave; non-restrictive criteria of admissibility for leave; financial structures that spread the financial risks among numerous partners; and flexibility of work hours.

Male-female equity

Anxo (2002), who studied the effects of daycare services in Sweden and in France, proposes that daycare centres encourage women to work not only by ensuring their children are cared for, but also by encouraging fathers to do more of the household tasks. Swedish mothers generally increase their professional activities when their children reach the age of three. At the same time, the fathers increase the amount of time they spend on domestic chores by 4.5 hours per week. According to Anxo, this shows the importance of daycare centres in encouraging a fair distribution of tasks between men and women, and professional activity by women.

According to the European Union study on European family-work balancing systems, the Nordic systems are oriented towards not only family welfare but also male-female equity. The fact that mothers work is very generally accepted and the model of the father as the family's sole support is strongly rejected. Moreover, this study shows that Sweden and the Netherlands are the countries in which, when it comes to the amount of time spent on daily domestic tasks, the disparities between men and women are the least.

Breastfeeding

According to another researcher (Galtry, 2003), even if the female employment rate in Sweden is very high, the rate of exclusive breastfeeding until the age of six months is also one of the highest in the industrialized countries. This suggests that, with adequate policies, it is possible to have, at the same time, many working mothers and many breastfeeding mothers. By encouraging a long period of breastfeeding the Swedish system indirectly

Credit: Dean Mitchell, IStock Photo

In Norway, mothers are entitled to two unpaid half-hours per day, for as long as they continue to breastfeed. They are also able to begin their workday an hour later or end it an hour earlier. As for employees of the national and municipal governments, their breastfeeding pauses and free hour are paid, and part-time employees are entitled to the same measures.

succeeds in realizing the known benefits of breastfeeding on children's health. According to Galtry, since daycare centres for nursing infants are not subsidized, the result of the Swedish model is that such infants stay at home for the first year of life, creating favourable conditions for prolonged breastfeeding. Other researchers note that the duration of parental leave affects the timing of the return to work: in 2011, the Swedes were slower in returning to work than the French, who had only four months of leave. The French also resumed full-time work more rapidly.

The wellbeing of mothers and children

In its 2014 annual State of the World's Mothers report, Save the Children compared the welfare of mothers and children in 178 countries, and listed Finland as the best place in the world to be a mother. Finland is in top place because it has strong performance across all five dimensions of maternal and child health and well-being: lifetime risk of maternal death, under-5 mortality rate, expected number of years of formal schooling, gross national income per capita, and participation of women in national government. Norway, Sweden, and Iceland occupy the second, third, and fourth places, and Denmark is in sixth place. Canada is in eighteenth place, and the United States in thirty-first. Sweden has been in first place eight times, Norway four and Finland twice.

Key ideas

Offering respite to single-parent families

The city of Stockholm offers a family support service which takes care of a single parent's child for one or two weekends per month so as to give a break to the parent … and sometimes also to the child.

Increasing the number of fathers on paternal leave

Increasing the number of fathers taking paternal leave is an explicit goal of the parental insurance agency in Sweden. Every year, all fathers receive letters reminding them of the number of available days that remain available to them and of the deadline for claiming these days. The main activity of the agency is diffusing publicity and information on fathers' rights to parental leave. These awareness-raising programs stress the positive effects of parental leave for both child and parent.

These benefits are also described in prenatal courses. Almost one hundred percent of parents expecting a first child attend such courses. Moreover, discussion groups for future fathers are available in several municipalities.

At the beginning of the 1990s, the government created the Papa Group, which rapidly became a major player in debates on parental leave for men. By the positions it took, mainly in the media, this group meant to influence attitudes on and representations of the role of fathers.

Guaranteed family allowance

Since 1917, single-parent families in Sweden receive a minimal family allowance from the state, which then claims the amount paid from the parent who does not have custody. When this amount cannot be collected from a parent, the state pays the allowance. Quebec has a similar policy for collecting alimony though, in the absence of the father, Quebec does not assume the costs. In Sweden, the amount of the allowance greater than the amount paid by the government must be paid directly by the parent who does not have custody to the other parent. This allowance plays an important role for families living in poverty by compensating for the financial resources lost when a spouse leaves the household and stops contributing to the pool of family resources.

Protecting women who work part-time

Given that most part-time workers are women, the Swedish government has proposed prohibiting discrimination towards part-time and contract employees in the following areas: salary conditions, retirement, work safety, social benefits, and training. Such a measure would reduce the penalization of women working part-time. It would also have the advantage of allowing women access to positions generally reserved for men who, traditionally, are less likely to work part-time or to think well of such work.

CHAPTER 6

Policies to Support Housing

Housing conditions can have major impacts on health. Mold, inadequate heating, insalubrious and polluted environments are just some of the problems that jeopardize physical health. Similarly, psychological health is threatened daily by noise, crowding, ghettoization, the unsettling effect of frequent moves, unsafe neighbourhoods, etc. Efforts to reduce social inequalities in health include fighting for access to decent housing.

Key policy principles

The housing policies of the Nordic countries are clearly distinct from those generally applied in other Western countries. They are based, first and foremost, on a fundamental principle: the right to housing for all. Moreover, they reflect a holistic vision of an ensemble of needs, seek to serve as a counterweight to the free market, and take a sustainable development perspective.

Housing, a right for all

The policies of housing assistance in the Scandinavian countries rest on the principle that all residents must have access to decent housing. Housing assistance is thus a central element in the social protection nets offered by governments. To the idea of the right to decent housing these policies add that of a right to a decent living environment. Eliminating homelessness is also a common and important objective of the housing policies of the Nordic countries. Measures dealing with homelessness are discussed in the section on social inclusion.

A holistic vision

The assistance programs are designed to encourage access to decent housing, not only to respect the universal right to housing; they are also motivated by a more global and simultaneously social and practical perspective. According to the Danish government, "[a] basic fact in the housing area is that general social improvement, including social inclusion, will not occur unless the physical framework is reasonably well maintained."[1]

An explicit counterweight to the free market

The governments of the Nordic countries wish to act so that even the least 'attractive' families on the residential market (such as those with children) have access to decent housing.

The prime aim of Finland's social housing program is "to create a stable housing market that is balanced between social classes and geographic regions."[2] This program also has the goal of "increasing the supply of modestly priced land to build on."

In Norway, the basic principle of the housing allowance system is that "a fixed share of the difference between actual housing expenses and reasonable income-dependent housing expenses is covered by the housing allowances."[3]

Many residences are protected from the vagaries of the market in Sweden and Denmark since a good deal of rental housing there is public, managed by municipal housing societies or other public agencies. In Sweden, public housing represents 20 percent of the housing stock. Moreover, 18 percent of homes are cooperatives; rents for cooperatives, however, are subject to the rules of the marketplace and are relatively high. In Denmark, 19 percent of housing is public.

---

1. Denmark Ministry of Social Welfare, Ministry of Interior Affairs and Health. *National Report on Strategies for Social Protection and Social Inclusion*, 2006, p. 23.
2. Finland Ministry of the Environment. "Housing", 2007. [www.environment.fi], free translation.
3. Nordvik, V. and P. Åhrén. *The Norwegian Housing Allowances–Efficiency and Effects*. Paper presented at the European Network for Housing Research conference, Cambridge, United Kingdom, 2004.

Credit: The Housing Association Ringgaarden

Eco-house 99, a complex of social and eco-friendly housing in Aarhus, Denmark. The governments of the Nordic countries take care to offer high-quality housing to people with low incomes. Visitors from other countries are often surprised by the architectural and functional quality of public housing.

Sustainable development

Housing policies, along with the overall strategies of urban and rural development, fit into the sustainable development perspective of assuring a habitat of high quality in the future. The agencies that implement housing policies in Sweden and Finland belong to the Ministries of the Environment. Sweden's National Board of Housing, Building and Planning, although an independent agency, is linked primarily to the Ministry of the Environment. In Finland, the Ministry of the Environment designs all housing policies, and the Housing Finance and Development Centre of Finland, a government agency, implements them.

Housing assistance measures

Government support for housing is consistent with the policies under discussion. Programs of housing benefits, and the different types of benefits, are designed to help those most in need. Here are several examples:

Credit: Cecilia Larsson/imagebank.sweden.se

The eco-neighborhood of Understenshöjden, which is also a cooperative, is located only four kilometers from the centre of Stockholm. The region's first eco-village was completed in 1996 and consists of 44 housing units of varying sizes, each supplied with solar panels and constructed of eco-friendly materials. It also has a community building equipped with a large kitchen and a playroom.

- In Norway, persons with low incomes have a right to housing benefits paid by the national government. The amount granted is a function of income and anticipated housing expense. There are also municipal benefits, for which retired and handicapped people are eligible, as well as individual benefits to help renters living in public housing.
- In Sweden, housing benefits are available for a range of recipients: families, households with shared custody of children, childless adults between the ages of 18 and 29, and the retired. The amount granted varies according to several criteria: cost and size of the residence, household income, and number of children.

- In Finland, benefits are granted to those with low incomes, and to both landlords and renters. Workers, the retired, and students are also eligible, so that they can be assured suitable housing. In Denmark, housing benefits are granted as a function of a combination of criteria: household makeup, income, and housing condition.

The Swedish example

Sweden has a long tradition of housing assistance: it launched its benefit program at the end of the 1940s, whereas most other countries did not launch their programs until the 1960s or 1970s. After a period of great generosity, characterized by a complete range of subsidies (income-based and non-income based, to landlords and to tenants, reduced interest rates), housing assistance evolved to resemble more closely the measures implemented in other European countries. Until the 1990s, everybody was eligible for public housing, and generous subsidies helped develop both private and public housing projects. Today, there are many conditions to be met. Despite cutbacks, housing assistance remains substantial: in 2007, 20 percent of Swedish households received a housing benefit, including 82 percent of all single-parent households and 23 percent of retired-person households.

Researchers have tried to determine whether the Swedish housing benefits system has created dependence on the welfare state. After analysing the dynamics resulting from receiving benefits during a ten-year period (from 1991 to 2002), they found no sign of dependence, even when they controlled for various socio-demographic characteristics of the beneficiaries, and tested various combinations of variables. According to the researchers, one cannot conclude that housing benefits encourage dependence, even when the benefit period is prolonged.

Public housing

Housing constructed to be accessible to all and to ensure that all are well lodged is called 'public' rather than 'social' housing. This is why in Sweden, for example, eligibility for public housing, until recently, did not depend on income. The quality of public housing offered is comparable to that offered by the private sector. The city of Stockholm now offers its renters the possibility of buying their apartments.

Public housing plays an important role in Sweden and Denmark, accounting for 20 percent of the residential market. In Norway, on the other hand, it only accounts for 6 percent of the market.

Key ideas

Avoid ghettoization

In 2004 a double strategy to counter ghettoization in social housing complexes was adopted in Denmark: stop building single-function installations, and promote socio-economic heterogeneity amongst the residents. Thus commercial and industrial companies were added to these housing complexes. Moreover, in 25 underprivileged neighbourhoods, local authorities were allowed to refuse housing applications from welfare recipients on the condition that the applicants were offered housing elsewhere. The authorities could also provide relocalization benefits to underprivileged residents who wanted to move away from problem neighbourhoods. Greater socio-economic mixing was also realized through another strategy: when a social housing unit became vacant, instead of trying to rent it, the authorities decided to sell it so as to bring less disadvantaged residents into the complex. The application of this double strategy was closely monitored by a council composed of representatives from the housing and business sectors and from the local authorities. This council had to continuously evaluate needs, initiatives, and pilot projects.

Revitalize disadvantaged neighbourhoods

Denmark has implemented grant programs to improve the quality of disadvantaged and old neighbourhoods. The process of revitalizing these neighbourhoods relies, in part, on residents' participation and suggestions. In a spirit of democracy and transparency, residents are consulted right from the start of each project and take part in all its stages, even the most specialized. For example, in one of these projects, residents (who were mostly students) asked that green technologies be integrated in the renovation of their neighbourhood. The municipality responded favourably. Thanks to this program, in ten years, twenty-three disadvantaged or old blocks were renovated and the quality of housing units improved. Today, these blocks have community rooms, re-greened yards, and bike racks. In Copenhagen, the capital, thanks to a similar program financed by the city and the central government, eighty blocks have, since 1997, been renovated and redeveloped.

CHAPTER 7

Gender Equity Policies

By definition, gender equity helps reduce social inequalities. Incontrovertibly women are enriched, both financially and as citizens, when they are included on an equal footing with men in all spheres of public life. Such inclusion also helps give access to interesting jobs to a large number of mothers in single- and two-parent families, and promotes the well-being of the entire family. Equality of men and women in the private sphere is just as important. Equity policies can contribute, notably by encouraging the desexualization of roles.

The key principles of gender equity policies

What distinguishes gender equity policies in the Nordic countries first and foremost is the extensive consensus support they receive from politicians, unions, and other organizations. These policies encourage equal opportunity and fight sexism starting at a very early age, and following an integrated approach.

A wide consensus

The Swedish parliament has unequivocally expressed its political position on the issue of gender equity. As the Swedish Institute points out: "Every year since 1994, the annual Statement of Government Policy has declared the conviction that a gender equality perspective must permeate all aspects of government policy."[1]

---

1. Swedish Institute. *Equality between women and men*, Fact sheet, 2004.

This consensus is also reflected in the allocation of management positions, which demonstrates what can be achieved in equity. Sweden and the other Nordic countries were pioneers in gender equity, legalizing votes for women in 1906 (Finland), 1913 (Norway), 1915 (Denmark), and 1919 (Sweden). In 2015, almost half of Swedish parliamentarians (45 percent) are women, and 12 of the 23 ministerial positions are held by women. (In Canada, 25 percent of MPPs (MNAs in Quebec) are women.) According to the Swedish government, this high percentage of female representation "is due to a firm conviction among all political parties concerning the need to increase the number of women candidates."[2] Since 1994, the largest party numerically, the Social Democratic party, has systematically run an equal number of male and female candidates at elections. It would seem, according to the United Nations, that imposing quotas is a particularly effective way of increasing the number of women in politics:

> A number of factors are at play in determining women's political representation – including political will, the strength of national women's movements and continued emphasis by the international community on gender equality and women's empowerment. However, the most decisive factor remains gender quota systems. In 2006, countries with quotas nearly doubled the number of women elected, compared to countries without any form of gender quota system.[3]

The most important political work in parliament is carried out by committees. In 2015, women hold between 41 and 59 percent of the seats on the nine parliamentary committees. In 2012, the OECD published data on the share of women on boards in listed companies: in Canada, this share is six percent; with 19 percent, Sweden comes second in the world after Norway (where the share is 38 percent). As far as management of national public organizations is concerned, measures have been implemented in Sweden to increase female representation. The percentage of managers in such organizations who are female rose from 16 percent in 1986 to 47 percent in 2001.

The other Nordic countries have also made notable progress in assuring that women have access to power. This, at least, is what the World Economic Forum (WEF) claims. It reports annually on gender equity, citing statistics on such indicators as the proportion of women who work, their incomes, the proportion of women managers and professionals, the

---

2. Swedish Institute. *Equality between women and men*, Fact sheet, 2004.
3. United Nations. *The Millenium Development Goals Report, 2007*, p. 13.

Credit: Cecilia Larsson/imagebank.sweden.se

In Sweden, an equity ombudsman whose task it is to make employers aware of the issue of equity and to educate them on it supports gender equity in the workplace. Equity begins at school, or even in daycare, where girls and boys are offered the same possibilities.

level of education of women, their health, and the proportion of women parliamentarians and ministers. According to the latest and the previous WEF annual reports, four Nordic countries — Iceland, Norway, Finland, and Sweden — have, for the last nine years, held the top four places in the world as ranked by such indicators. Denmark comes in seventh place.

Equal opportunity

There is ample evidence that gender equity is widely perceived in Nordic societies as a necessity. Moreover, current policies encourage equal opportunity by promoting financial autonomy, the desexualization of roles, and power and influence for women.

Financial autonomy for women is encouraged by policies designed to develop each person's capacity to achieve economic independence through employment income. Measures for balancing work and family life, to give just one example, support these policies.

The desexualization of roles is made concrete by policies allowing each person to participate in all aspects of private and public life, including participating in life as a citizen. Statistics Sweden affirms that "women and men shall take the same responsibility for household work and shall have the same opportunities to give and receive care on equal terms."[4]

Individual and collective power and influence are manifestations of equal opportunities, for both men and women, to take charge of one's life and influence society. As Statistics Sweden puts it: "The overall objective for gender equality policy is to ensure that women have equal power to shape society and their own lives. (…) this implies (…) an equal distribution of power and influence. Women and men shall have the same rights and opportunities to be active citizens and be able to form the terms of decision making."[5]

Preventing sexism

Gender equity is an objective for daycares and for all levels of the educational system — that is, just as much for the schools attended by youth from 7 to 16 years old (equivalent to primary and secondary schools in Quebec) as for postsecondary institutions. As the Swedish Institute puts it

---

4. Statistics Sweden (2014). *Women and Men in Sweden; Facts and Figures 2014*, page 3.
5. Ibid., page 3.

Credit: Ulf Huett Nilsson/imagebank.sweden.se

"Teachers .. must understand the impact of gender on learning processes." Swedish Institute. *Equality between women and men.*

on its website: "Studies show that girls' and boys' classroom behaviour and study choices differ. If teachers are to promote equality, they must therefore understand the impact of gender on learning processes and integrate this into their teaching skills."[6]

The key idea in the policy as applied to the school system is that sexualized roles are obstacles. Young people have the right to become free-thinking individuals, to develop in full liberty, to use all their capacities regardless of their sex. They have the right to become open-minded people, capable of critical, independent thought. They even have the right to question their parents' system of values.

In this perspective, the role of daycares and schools is to provide a sanctuary where children can develop their own personalities, free of pressure from media and advertising. Likewise, their mission is to protect children from the unjustified influence of certain family milieus.

6. Swedish Institute. *Equality between women and men*, Fact sheet, 2004.

The integrated approach

The design of gender equality policies follows an integrated approach, according to which the principle of equality extends to all other policies. Thus equality policies determine goals which all ministries and government agencies must take into consideration in developing and implementing their own policies. 'Gender mainstreaming' are the terms used to designate this concept. The following extract from a Danish ministerial report shows precisely what this means:

> The Danish Gender Equality Act provides that public authorities must within their respective areas of responsibility seek to promote equal opportunities and incorporate gender equality in all planning and administration. To fulfil this obligation, comprehensive cross-ministerial work has been ongoing for several years, the aim being to create new tools and methods for gender equality work.[7]

The Danish government has created tools for evaluating gender equality in its laws, communications, and campaigns, in the allocation of resources, and in the production of separate data and statistics on men and women. Every new law is assessed to determine whether or not it needs to be submitted for a complete evaluation from the perspective of gender equality.

In Sweden, different government offices oversee the application of the gender equity policy.

1. The Division for Gender Equality is responsible for supporting the ministries in integrating the gender equality perspective in all policies. It trains government authorities and public service agents on matters of equality and collaborates with international organizations on such questions. It also assures that there is equal representation of men and women among state employees. It is responsible for coordinating the government's work on gender equality, special gender equality initiatives and development of methods to implement the Government's gender equality policy.
2. The Equality Ombudsman, an independent public institution, checks to see that the law against discrimination and the Parental Leave Act are respected. For instance, it seeks to ensure that employees on parental leave are not treated less favourably at work,

7. Denmark, Ministry of Socal Affairs, Ministry of Interior Affairs and Health. *National Report on Strategies for Social Protection and Social Inclusion*, 2006, p. 6.

and it monitors how employers and education institutions live up to the provisions of the Discrimination Act.

3. The Committee on Discrimination "can demand employers and education providers to take active measures against discrimination, for example based on gender, and levy fines for non-compliance."

4. The county administrative board of each of Sweden's twenty-one counties includes a regional expert in gender equality issues. This expert promotes the integration of the gender-equality approach and supports equality efforts in his or her region.

Sweden dedicates significant financial resources to the advancement of equality between men and women. At the time of the 2010 municipal and county elections, the Swedish government allocated the equivalent of CAN$22 million to support the equality program. The government then added $12 million to prolong its support from 2011 to 2013. Moreover, it has invested $2 million to help the work done by government agencies using the integrated approach by commissioning a study from the Swedish Secretariat for Gender Research at the University of Gothenburg. The goal of this study is to further develop integrated-approach methods, to create a forum for discussion of related experiences, to supply information, and to create conditions supporting this approach in the long term.

The Swedish law banning the purchase of sexual services, which punishes clients but not prostitutes, clearly represents a very advanced form of the struggle for gender equality. This law recognizes that most prostitutes live in very difficult social conditions. It aims to fight prostitution, which since it is currently linked to large-scale crime, trafficking in women, and the drug trade, is harmful not only for individuals but also for society in general. Buying or trying to buy sexual services by paying money or by some other exchange (with drugs or alcohol, for instance) is punishable by a fine or by up to a year in jail. On the other hand, selling sexual services is not a crime. An enquiry looking into the issue estimated that street prostitution has dropped fifty percent since the law came into effect in 1999, that prostitution offered elsewhere or on the internet has not increased, and that this law also plays an important role in preventing human trafficking.

Key ideas

Take adequate measures

In conformity with the integrated approach described above, the Swedish government has introduced two measures. The first obliges all commissions of inquiry to include an evaluation of the impact of the subject of their inquiry on equality between men and women. The second measure concerns Statistics Sweden. In order to give an account of realities for women and men, this organization must disaggregate official statistics by sex. This is how the organization sees its role in striving for an egalitarian world:

> Women and men should be visible in the statistics. For this to be possible, statistics must be disaggregated by sex. The Swedish Parliament has decided that gender statistics are to be a part of the official statistics. The goal is that all statistics concerning individuals shall not only be collected, analysed and presented by sex, but also reflect gender issues and problems in society. Sex should be the basis for a comprehensive and thorough breakdown of all statistics.[8]

Adapt academic programs

At the post-secondary level (the equivalent of CEGEPs in Quebec) Sweden has reorganized a number of typically masculine programs in order to make them more attractive for women. For example, technology and science programs have been merged.

In schools, courses that are usually chosen by one sex more than the other — such as the traditionally masculine courses in technology and woodworking, and the traditionally feminine ones in housekeeping and sewing — are now obligatory for girls as well as for boys.

Moreover, the offering of courses for girls has been modified. They can now take unisex classes in the natural sciences, unisex summer courses in technology, and workshops in mechanics for women. As well, schools encourage visits from women who work in what are called 'male' occupations.

Helping women do 'men's' jobs

Given that men and women work in different sectors and practice distinct professions within the same sectors, the Swedish government has decided

---

8. Statistics Sweden. *Women and Men in Sweden; Facts and Figures 2014*, 2014, page 6.

to take steps to reinforce the position of women in the job market and in training programs. To this end, the government offers assistance programs for women who launch their own businesses (investments totaling US$4.3 million over three years). It has implemented other measures as well, such as training in computer science and in economics designed for women; projects to increase the number of women in so-called 'male' professions; support for women in workplaces dominated by men; mentorship in career planning; and subsidized orientation programs for unemployed women.

Increase the power of women from other cultures

The population of Sweden includes a minority of 'gypsy' origin, now known as the Roma or Romanies. The culture of these people is traditionally dominated by men. Networks for Roma women have been created to encourage them to participate actively in Roma organizations. Moreover, a working group has been set up which includes representatives of the government and Roma women with the aim of encouraging their political involvement.

CHAPTER 8

Education Policies

Education has a predominant place in the Nordic countries. Not surprisingly, it is free, of high quality, and accessible to all. Some of these countries' education systems are almost entirely public. Less than two percent of students attend private primary or secondary schools in Norway and three percent in Finland. In Sweden, the rate of for-profit and non-profit private schools rose from four percent in 2003 to fourteen percent in 2012. In Denmark, the rate is about 24 percent, again for both non-profit and for-profit private schools. Schubert and Martens (2005) described the Nordic approach to educational matters well:

> Denmark, Sweden and Finland are the EU countries with the largest public investments in education. They top the latest statistics: Denmark with 8.5% of GDP, Sweden with 7.66% and Finland with 6.24%, as against the EU average of 5.1%. But the Nordic approach to education is not just quantitative. Its qualitative aspect is just as important and particular. Education is not only seen as a privilege, but also as a right and a duty. It is the foundation of people's lives, no matter what their background or career prospects. Education facilities from kindergartens to universities are therefore free. The rationale of the system is that we cannot afford to lose even one pupil from the system. The positive results of the principle of equal rights and access to education are reflected directly in the know-how and productivity of the workforce. This ensures a high degree of competitiveness in times of change and the ability to adapt to new conditions and circumstances.[1]

---

1. Buhigas Schubert, C. and H. Martens. *The Nordic model: A recipe for European success?*, European Policy Centre, Brussels, 2005, p. 54.

According to OECD figures published in 2014, educational expenditure as a percentage of GDP in the Nordic countries is now between 6.2 and 7.5 percent, with the EU average being 5.3 percent.

Several studies have highlighted the success of the Swedish preschool system. The aims of Quebec's childcare centres (*Centres de la petite enfance*, CPE), like those of the Swedish system, are to offer high quality, affordable, and accessible service. The latter, well integrated into a comprehensive educational system and noted for the pedagogic quality and for flexibility both in financial and geographic terms, serves as an inspiring example for the former. Hence the interest in studying the Swedish preschool system.

The Finnish school system has been an impressive success for several reasons. First, dropping out of school is virtually nonexistent in Finland. Only one percent of Finns do not earn a secondary school diploma. More than 90 percent of them carry on studying at higher levels (professional and other training), and 33 percent go to university. Moreover, the literacy and numeracy rates in Finland are both in second place in the world after Japan, according to the first OECD PIAAC survey (Programme for the International Assessment of Adult Competencies) published in 2013.

Secondly, the quality of education in Finland is exceptionally high. According to the OECD's PISA tests, designed to evaluate the school systems of its member countries, secondary-school students in Finland do better than those in other countries, and do so in many subjects. In a 2003 evaluation of 41 countries, students from Finland were at the top of the list in reading and, along with students from Japan and Korea, in mathematics and sciences. In 2006, Finnish students topped the rankings in the sciences. In 2009, they were ranked best in the Western world and, after students in China and Korea, best in the world.

Thirdly, of all the western countries, the achievement gap — the disparity between schools in academic results — is lowest in Finland. In 2006, the four Nordic countries (including Iceland) were ranked among the top eight for lowest achievement gap. These results show that equality of opportunity from adolescence on (and doubtless from well before) really does exist in the Nordic countries; these countries continue to create societies with minimal social and health inequalities.

The Swedish preschool system

The Scandinavian model, under construction for sixty years, shows remarkable resilience. One of the pillars of the model, clearly, is a well-developed family policy whose provisions include an extensive network of educational, affordable, and high-quality childcare services. A brief outline of the key elements of the Swedish preschool system will be particularly relevant and illuminating in light of Quebec's network of Centres de la Petite Enfance (CPE), for Quebec's ambitious effort shares goals with the inspiring Swedish system.

Daycares in Sweden are part of an educational whole, completely integrated into the school structure. Significant budgetary resources are dedicated to them. In 2006, the Swedish childcare service was one of the most, if not the most, costly of state programs with a budget 50 billion kronor (CAN$7 billion), some two to three percent of GDP.

The family policy context

In Sweden, the preschool educational system falls within the larger framework of a rigorous and highly developed family policy. The main elements of this policy are the following:

- Generous parental insurance
- Long periods of parental leave
- Accessibility to high-quality childcare services
- An extensive range of educational services to help families, including free preparatory classes for primary school, and numerous libraries well stocked with children's books
- Urban planning measures and transport policies favourable to families such as transport adapted for strollers, numerous playgrounds, pedestrian zones, and very numerous green spaces
- Specific job market measures, such as the possibility of working part time
- Benefits of all sorts, such as help for children who are sick or who have special needs, or for parents who are single or students.

The objective of the family policy is, by promoting the well-being not only of families but also of parents on the one hand and children on the other, to create conditions that favour paternity, maternity, and the education of children. According to this policy, parental well-being requires that both the father and the mother strike a balance between work and family responsibilities. In consequence, the policy allows both parents equal access to the job market and encourages fair sharing of family responsibilities. As we saw in Chapter 7, this vision runs counter to the model of the family

Credit: Martin Svalander/imagebank.sweden.se

Swedish law limits the cost of daycare so that all parents can benefit from preschool daycare services. Laws act in several ways to encourage the development of children and to protect them. In 1979, for example, Sweden was the first country to pass a law making spanking a crime.

in which the man is the sole provider. Thus by offering parental leave of 480 days, freely divided between the father and the mother (except for two months of the total leave period reserved exclusively for each parent), the state helps parents spend time with their young children. The parental leave also offers the financial possibility of reducing work hours until such time as the child has reached the age of eight.

As well as contributing to social solidarity, a positive feature of the social-democratic model, the childcare services also offer young children many clear advantages, not the least of which is the chance to interact and socialize with a diverse range of other kids. The organizational structure on which the system relies is worth describing.

The structure of the Swedish school system

Young Swedes follow an academic path unlike the one we are familiar with in Quebec. The story of Åsa, a girl from Stockholm, typifies the experience of the majority of young Swedes. (Figure 8.1 illustrates this typical academic path.)

> Åsa stayed at home from birth until she was 18 months old. She was with her mother until her first birthday, and with her father for the following six months. Starting at 14 months, she occasionally attended a drop-in nursery centre for several hours at a time. This service was provided under a program known as "open daycare." When she was almost 18 months old she gradually began attending a regular daycare, part-time at first, and then full time. The daycare centre was in her neighbourhood, ten minutes on foot from her home. It cost her parents 60 kroner per day (about $8). Once she was three years old, the costs of daycare dropped. Åsa, like all Swedish children, is entitled to 525 hours of free daycare per year. At the age of 5, Åsa still attended the daycare centre fulltime, but she spent about ten hours every week at the primary school, becoming familiar with the school environment. This prep-aratory-class service is available to all, and free. When she was six, she began going to primary school fulltime. When school ended, she spent two hours at the school's daycare centre.

Daycare services are thus completely integrated into the school system and, like the schools, are administered by the Ministry of Education. Responsibility for daycares was transferred from Sweden's Ministry for Social Affairs in 1998. In Quebec, daycare services are the responsibility of the Ministère de la Famille, and schools the responsibility of the Ministère de l'Éducation. Moreover, daycare centres in Sweden are designated as *förskolor*, Swedish for 'preschool institutions'.

The National Agency for Education, a branch of the Ministry of Education, oversees the entire Swedish school system. It is responsible for planning programs, and defines standards and general directions for all levels of the system, from daycares to universities.

The mandate of the Swedish Schools Inspectorate is to control the quality of all educational services, from those for infants to those for adults, and to publish qualitative reports on themes such as the development of competencies in children of preschool age. The types of inspections carried out are numerous: they range from auto-evaluation to external evaluation, and include surveys of children and of their parents. The National Agency for Education and the Swedish Schools Inspectorate enjoy considerable autonomy relative to the Ministry of Education.

Daycares are managed by municipalities, which play a role comparable to that played by school boards in Quebec. As well as acting as employers,

FIGURE 8.1

The Swedish preschool system

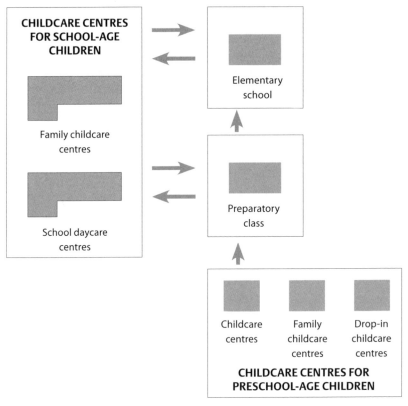

Source: skolverket.se

municipalities are responsible for ensuring that new daycares are accredited. The central government allocates a budgetary envelope to municipalities which, in using daycare funding, have enjoyed more room to maneuver since 1998 than was previously the case.

History of daycare services

The success of the Swedish preschool system, as highlighted by several studies, is the achievement of several decades of evolution. The system is characterized by sustained and rapid growth, high quality, deregulation, and decentralization.

At the beginning of the 1970s the services offered were piecemeal and discriminatory. There were orphanage-type nurseries attended full-time by the children of single working mothers; and there were stimulating kindergartens where middle-class and upper-class kids, who spent most of their time at home with their mothers, spent a few hours per day playing and socializing. It was during this period, nevertheless, that widely accessible public daycare service began to develop. The intent of the 'new' daycares was to encourage the well-being of children and social mixing, and to support parents' professional activities.

In 1975, about 60,000 children were enrolled in Swedish daycares. This number grew rapidly and continuously during the following fifteen years, encouraging the massive integration of women into the job market. The total budget for daycare exploded, going from 2.9 billion kroner to 25 billion kroner (more than CAN$5 billion) in the period 1975 to 1990.

Meanwhile, at the beginning of the 1980s, the preschool system, which had been very normative and quite centralized, evolved into a deregulated and decentralized system and did so without worsening of its pedagogic quality. The standards in force, defined at the central level by the Agency for Social Affairs, determined the educator-to-child radio and the area of playgrounds. At a time when the country was in an economic downturn, these standards were considered obstacles to the growth of daycares and the control of costs. In 1984, Olof Palme's Social Democratic Party abolished the standards, simplified the pedagogic program, and decentralized responsibilities by transferring them to municipalities. In conformity with the law, this deregulation must not lead to deterioration in the quality of services. Quite the contrary, in fact, for the goal was to rely more on the competencies of daycare centres and of educators. Municipalities experienced enormous pressure to create new daycare places quickly, to find qualified staff, who were very much in demand, and to track down adequate premises. As well, to maintain the high quality of services, the Ministry of Education eventually implemented the means of control and evaluation mentioned above.

The growth of the network was interrupted by the economic crisis of the 1990s, which caused, notably, an increase in the rate of unemployment — a significant increase for a country used to full employment — and the devaluation of the Swedish krona. Cutbacks in public expenditures led to a reduction in the quality of the services: the number of children in each care group went up, the ratio of educators to children went down, and the costs of daycare exploded. Many parents then decided to look after their children at home.

The economic recovery that followed allowed a response to the heightened demand. Starting in 1993, the state began to offer quasi-complete coverage of the soaring needs. A noteworthy fact: 95 percent of children between three and five years old now attend daycare.

The rising curve of daycare attendance in Figure 8.2 (from 1993) can be explained by catching up and by demographic factors. Nonetheless, what this graph charts — an average annual increase of 20 percent — is a remarkable development. In 2010 there were more than 400,000 daycare places for a population of nine million, compared to some 200,000 places in Quebec's CPEs.

There is now debate about the choice between a normative approach as opposed to deregulation. On the one hand, from the point of view of assuring pedagogic quality, the normative approach is not necessarily a panacea. Some consider that university training for educators, adequate financing, a good pedagogic program, integration within the Ministry of

FIGURE 8.2

Number of registrations in Swedish daycare centers – 1975-2008

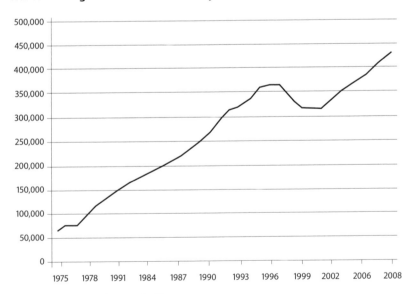

Source: Swedish National Agency for Education

Education, and a territorial approach also constitute assurances of quality. On the other hand, deregulation raises several concerns, given that some municipalities have modified ratios and the size of child groups. Be that as it may, deregulation of daycare services constitutes a path to follow only for services that have reached full maturity, as is the case in Sweden, and for those that can count on educators having a high level of competence.

Key ideas

The main elements of the Swedish preschool system are, in fact, the keys to its success. They offer food for thought. Better yet, they are a source of inspiration for the future development of Quebec's preschool system.

Integrate daycare services into the educational system

The integration of daycare services into the educational system, at the levels both of legislation and of municipal planning and management, allows such services to be treated as places of learning, like schools where children learn through play, with a distinct pedagogy.

This approach offers the advantage of assuring transversal coherence in education, and doing so no matter what the type of organization. Whether the students are three-year olds, or 55-year-olds enrolled in an adult-education program, it gives education a valuable and central role in society.

The transfer of the responsibility for daycare services from the Ministry of Social Affairs to the Ministry of Education seems to have been well received by the great majority of those involved. This was confirmed by two national evaluations, which were carried out five and ten years after the reform.

Separate planning and control functions

The separation of the National Educational Agency, which defines standards and programs, from the Swedish Schools Inspectorate, the organization that inspects the work of daycare services and oversees the application of the law, is a key point. The distinct missions of the two organizations create the needed space between, on the one hand, the authority to define rules and standards, and on the other, the authority to ensure these standards and rules are respected.

Adopt a territorial approach

The more municipalities have room to maneuver in managing daycare services, the more easily they can meet needs.

For several years, the subsidy granted for daycare services has not been subject to precise objectives. The municipalities have been free to use the funds as they please. In decentralizing — in giving municipalities greater authority — the Ministry of Education considers that it allows daycare services to adapt better to community needs, and municipalities to manage in a more integrated fashion both daycare services and schools, for which they are also responsible. Moreover, given that the municipalities compete to attract young families to their territories, they make a considerable effort to offer attractive daycare services.

As we have already mentioned, some consider that decentralization and diversification of services represent a risk for maintaining quality in all municipalities, particularly if one takes into account the low population density in isolated regions such as Lapland. There are reported cases of municipalities making budgetary choices detrimental to the quality of services, notably by reducing the ratio of educators to children. In general, however, many people agree that the advantages (integrated management adapted to the local realities, competition between municipalities to attract young families) outweigh the disadvantages.

Securely connect daycare services to the school environment

The Swedes have found at least two ways to link daycare services to the school environment: first, by establishing preparatory classes, and second, by encouraging a single management structure for both daycares and schools. For example, when we visited the municipality of Nacka, a suburb of Stockholm, we met one school principal who was simultaneously responsible for a school and for several daycares.

In Quebec, the lack of ties between the CPEs and the schools is a deficiency often noted … and lamented.

Communicate directly with parents

The use of new technologies allows educators to communicate directly with parents about the development of their children. At the Nacka daycare, for example, there are computers in every room. As the director explained:

The educators have access to several ways of communicating with the parents. They use email, photos, and films. They are professionals. The better the communication, the better the daycare. Today, parents also know more about the work educators do, for they themselves went through daycares when they were little. The private meetings between parents and the educator are very important. Now, rather than just mentioning little details of the day, educators can better inform parents about what their child is learning and how he or she is developing. They have access to several tools for doing so.[2]

Develop the teaching skills of staff

Educators (known in Swedish as 'preschool teachers') with a wide range of competencies are one of the main components of Swedish daycare services. They have university training and receive salaries comparable to those of primary school teachers. Their pedagogic competencies allow them to concentrate on teaching, while 'teachers' aides' look after the children's basic needs. In practice, however, the functions performed by staff in both these professional categories often overlap.

Recruiting certified educators remains a challenge for several municipalities, for such educators are in high demand and 50 percent of the staff in daycare centres have a university diploma. The salaries and competencies clearly reflect the fact that this is a highly valued educational profession. Moreover the overhaul of the national pedagogic program in 2011 stressed the underutilization of the educators' competencies and proposed to give them a leadership role relative to other professional categories. Despite the progressive professionalization of daycare services, the Ministry of Education does not want its daycare services to depart from their distinguishing trait, learning through play.

Offer accessible and diversified daycare services

The population's expectations as to accessibility to daycare services are so great that the law stipulates that municipalities must guarantee that, within three to four months of a request being made for a place in a daycare, such a place will be available. In practice, almost all municipalities, with few exceptions, respect this obligation. Moreover, the offer of "open daycare"

---

2. Cited in Chartrand, S. *Les leçons du système préscolaire suédois*, rapport de recherche, Centre de recherche Léa-Roback sur les inégalités sociales de santé, Montreal, 2011, p. 12.

includes fifteen hours free for children between three and five years old, a measure that assures even greater access.

In addition to the municipal daycares, though less common, there are also cooperatives run by parents, private daycares, and family daycares. The centre-right governments of recent years have decided to offer parents a range of formulas, including childcare allowance. For some time now, there has been an observable increase in the proportion of childcare places reserved in the private and non-profit sectors.

Nevertheless, diversification of the services offered is part of the lively political debate on freedom of choice which has being going on between the centre right and the social democrats for more than twenty years. While the former favour the childcare benefit introduced in 2006, which allows parents to stay at home with their children, the latter prefer daycare services. But, first and foremost, this debate raises the question of freedom for parents to choose between daycare service and stay home with their children.

When it comes to childcare services, the Swedish example is unquestionably a model to be followed by any country that wants to offer its preschool-age children an educational milieu of high quality. Sweden's success in this realm is the result of unremitting effort to reach qualitative and quantitative objectives that would be unreachable without sizeable investments. This development clearly illustrates how Sweden has adopted a coherent approach in training pre-school teachers and in integrating daycare and preschool educational services along with primary and secondary schools into a consistent macrosystem under a single ministry.

The Finnish school system

One of the reasons for the success of the Finnish educational system, other than the main thrusts of the Finnish government's educational policy, is the Finns' attitude to school and reading.

As well, three characteristics of the Finnish education context should be taken into account. The first is that almost the entire educational system is public. Only about one percent of primary and secondary schools are private. For higher levels of education, this percentage climbs to less than four percent. The second characteristic is the following: municipalities are responsible for administering schools. The third characteristic concerns teaching: primary-school courses are given in the same establishment as secondary-school courses, and this school is close to students' homes.

The importance of the school

It should be mentioned right away that Finns think of school as an institution dedicated to success, and that all social classes value education. "The view of school is the same in all strata of the population."[3] Each student counts, for the state thinks of the country economy: Finland having a small population (5.5 million), each inhabitant counts and hence, each student. "Students in Finland are supported by the people around them, by their parents and teachers, and by policies."[4]

The Finns do not stint on teacher training: it takes five years to become qualified. Moreover, the profession is highly valued. The quotas controlling admission to the Faculties of Education are almost as restrictive as those for entering the Faculties of Medicine. Moreover, teachers benefit from specific training on learning difficulties. And continuing education is always available to them.

Respect for children

The state makes sure no child is forced prematurely into school by establishing the school starting age at seven. A child's rhythms and individuality are granted considerable respect. According to Devos and Meskel-Cresta (2004), "All students in Finland have a place in the system, and everything is done to help them find their place." Rather than flaunting their knowledge, teachers take time to observe their students. "They keep themselves in the background, behind the knowledge they transmit, and the educational material they use to do so."[5]

Special education

The Finnish educational system guarantees that every child will be offered excellent conditions for learning, and that no-one will be left on the sidelines. To help them overcome learning difficulties, 18 percent of all students (almost one in five) benefit from special education services within their own schools. It is thought that early interventions are ideal for overcoming such difficulties.

---

3. Devos, L. and M. Meskel-Cresta. *À la découverte du système éducatif finlandais*, Finnish Embassy to France, 2004, free translation.
4. Ibid., free translation.
5. Ibid., free translation.

The Finnish researchers Jahnukainen, Jyrkämä, and Takala (2001), specialists in the field of education, reckon that interventions to deal with educational problems contribute to preventing not only early school leaving but also exclusion from the job market and from society. They studied the path that begins with difficulties in school and ends with social exclusion, and defined the 'hierarchy' of exclusion:

- Stage 1: Difficulties encountered at school or at home by the child.
- Stage 2: Educational exclusion — the student fails in school, or drops out.
- Stage 3: Exclusion from work — the person experiences difficulties in the job market.
- Stage 4: Low level of education, unemployment, poverty — the person belongs to a disadvantaged subculture.
- Stage 5: Criminality, alcoholism, drug addiction — in the culmination of exclusion, the person belongs to a deviant subculture, and this may lead to incarceration or institutionalization.

According to Jahnukainen (2001), special educational services make great sense in the current context of a competitive job market, in which the links between education level and job situation become increasingly obvious. For those with little education, jobs are few and often short-term and badly paid.

Preparation for life

The aim of school is to produce, after years of schooling, youth capable of self-development or, in other words, youth that have learned how to learn. During this process the emphasis is on developing self-esteem. Once adulthood is reached, life-long learning, particularly through continuing education, is encouraged, and constitutes an essential element in the national education policy.

Economic equality

Lack of money should not be an obstacle to success in studies. Financial aid is provided to needy students in primary and secondary schools, and a free midday meal is served to all. Both textbooks and school transport are free.

The system is designed so that everyone can undertake post-secondary studies or receive professional training. Whether they are attending a

Credit: Graur Razvan Ionut/FreeDigitalPhotos.net

University is free in the Nordic countries, as in certain other European countries. In Finland and Sweden all students automatically have access to substantial loans and scholarships, which frees them from having to work while also studying.

FIGURE 8.3

Average tuition fees vs. the percentage of students receiving public subsidies for higher education, 2008-09

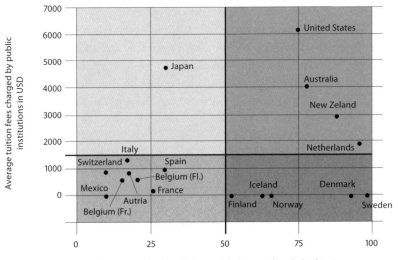

Note: Chart excludes OECD countries for which specific data on public subsidies is not available.

Source: OECD (2012). "How are Countries Around the World Supporting Students in Higher Education?" *Education Indicators in Focus*, No. 2, OECD Publishing, Paris.

pre-university college, receiving professional training, or going to university, students can claim financial help, housing allowances, or state-guaranteed loans. According to Devos and Meskel-Cresta (2004), "The authorities are obliged to organize equal opportunities for everyone to benefit from additional training and self-development according to their abilities and needs, and unhindered by their lack of financial means."[6] The state also intervenes to reduce inequalities between neighbourhoods: the poorer neighbourhoods receive the larger subsidies. The diagram above compares aid granted to university students in the Nordic countries with that granted in other countries.

6. Ibid.

Key ideas

Factors in the success of Finnish students

The Finnish National Board of Education identifies two key factors explaining the success of Finnish students: the society's strong support for reading and language learning; and the administration of schools at the local level, which means that teachers can enjoy both flexibility and adequate support. The board also notes the following education success factors: considerable individualized support for students, equal opportunities offered to all; well trained and highly autonomous teachers, and the application of the theory of social constructivism to learning.

Devos and Meskel-Cresta (2004) propose additional explanations. Finland, according to these authors, is a very homogeneous society. It is one of the OECD countries with the narrowest socio-economic gaps. Moreover, immigration is relatively limited. This facilitates the task of assuring everybody has an equal opportunity to succeed and the means to do so. These authors, like the Board of Education, note that the importance attached to reading is a major factor. Finnish families, they report, value reading and encourage the very young to learn to read. They also note that libraries are well stocked.

When it comes to learning difficulties, these authors observed several measures promoting student success. Teachers, for example, receive all the help they need from specialists; catch-up lessons are an obligatory part of teachers' tasks and, when needed, extra teachers can be assigned to give them.

Organizing exchanges between decision-makers and youth and their parents

The city of Helsinki values the participation of students and their parents in improving education. This is why the municipal authorities have set up The Voice of the Young in Helsinki, a project which includes open forums allowing young people to influence the development of their school environment.

The central goal of these forums is to promote dialogue between young people and decision-makers on important social issues. The forums are for all students between 13 and 18 years of age attending secondary schools or colleges or taking professional training, as well as for youth attending youth centres. Every year, four day-long forums are organized, each in a different neighbourhood of the city. These forums are called 'open' because members of the general public are welcomed during a two-hour period.

CHAPTER 9

Policies of Social Inclusion

In its document entitled *Towards Public Health on Equal Terms*, the Swedish Ministry of Health and Social Affairs mentions that the structure of society influences the health of individuals. It adds that there is ample scientific documentation of the links between health on the one hand, and social power and inclusion on the other. Prevention of social exclusion and measures to support those already excluded can have positive effects on health and well-being in several ways; for example, by indirectly affecting children in the care of adults who are excluded or at risk of being excluded.

The Norwegian government's national strategy for reducing social inequalities in health declares the following: amongst young people and children, social exclusion and poverty engender stress and difficult living conditions. They are associated with poor nutrition, delays in development (particularly language skills), failure in school, emotional problems, behavioural problems, lack of social skills, and poor self-esteem.

This chapter focuses on the basic principles of policies of social inclusion in general, and policies for including handicapped persons, immigrants, and the homeless in particular.

Key policy principles

By 'policies of social inclusion,' the Nordic countries' governments mean any policy aimed at the social integration of any individual, including those experiencing difficulties that harm their functioning in society (handicapped persons, drug addicts, the poor, the unemployed, and the homeless), or those who are going through a difficult period in their lives or are less available for work (such as the parents of young children, natural care-givers, or students) and are hence financially vulnerable.

According to this definition, all policies whose measures aim at protecting the incomes of individuals — no matter what difficulties these individuals are experiencing (employment insurance would be an example of such a measure) or their stage in life (paid parental leave, financial aid for students, or old age pension, for instance) — are considered as policies of social inclusion. It should be noted that the governments of the Nordic countries do not always distinguish between strategies of social inclusion and measures of social protection.

Political action based on an inter-sectoral approach

The governments of the Nordic countries favour an inter-sectoral approach to political action. Moreover, they consider that strategies of inclusion and social protection are the mandate of policies addressing distinct questions such as education, housing, jobs, family violence, and prostitution. Childcare, the flexibility offered to new parents as to when they return to work, and gender equity — to name just these concerns — are considered as the concerns of complementary policies.

Inclusion for all requires jobs for all

In the Nordic countries, access to jobs is at the heart of the strategies for including marginalized persons, immigrants, women, and young people — in short, all members of society.

In Sweden, "participation in the job market remains the main way of fighting against exclusion: professional training and continuing education, keeping a decent income (...) The Swedish strategy for fighting poverty remains so deeply linked to the strategy for promoting employment that it is sometimes difficult to distinguish between the two."[1]

In Denmark, "as a natural consequence of this active line in the social and employment strategies, the Danish 'Reform programme for growth and employment' as well as the 'National report on strategies for social protection and social inclusion' complement each other, striving to ensure that nobody is left on the fringes of the labour market or society. To this end, all the relevant ministries are working closely together to prepare the two instruments."[2]

---

1. PolitiquesSociales.net. « Suède – Note synthèse », 2006. [www.politiquessociales.net], free translation.
2. Denmark. Ministry of Social Welfare. Ministry of Interior Affairs and Health. *National Report on Strategies for Social Protection and Social Inclusion*, 2006, p. 3.

Holding a job contributes to autonomy and economic independence and prevents poverty. Moreover, holding a job offers several possibilities that favour social inclusion. These include:

Benefiting from everybody's potential

Even those who are most disadvantaged in terms of employability are considered to have resources and competencies from which society in general could benefit. The government needs to continue "activities aimed at paving the way for attaching these groups to the labour market"[3] even if this means, for example, offering handicapped persons work adapted to their capacities, or implementing measures for balancing the personal and professional lives of people caring for their relatives or of parents of young children. Governments clearly favour flexibility of work hours as a mode of integration.

Reducing social inequalities

Maximizing the number of people with jobs allows inequalities to be reduced, especially in the Nordic countries which, of all the countries in the West, have the narrowest spread in employment income.

Promoting citizen participation

Every citizen should be able to participate in all aspects of active life, and holding a job helps to this end. This perspective entails the right to work, and the right to continuing education so as to remain employable.

Creating the wealth needed for universal social protection

Employment is indeed an inclusion strategy, in a system in which a high rate of employment coupled with a high rate of income tax supplies the financial resources needed to guarantee that just because someone does not work temporarily or permanently, they will not be excluded from society. A large active population allows wealth to be redistributed among all individuals.

In the same spirit, there is an implicit social contract between the private sector and the government by virtue of which each party tries to

---

3. Ibid., p. 3.

respect the other's point of view. Thus state action is generally in step with that of the productive sector. For example, the state invests significantly in research and development (1.09 percent of GDP in Finland, 1.03 percent in Sweden and 0.99 percent in Denmark in 2011, more than in any other of sixteen major advanced economies.[4]) The state allows the private sector considerable freedom of action. Liberalism characterizes the labour legislation, while respecting the collective agreements of unions, in order to encourage productivity. On the other hand, the private sector accepts the high fiscal levies designed to prevent social exclusion.

Universality of access to nature and public transit

Integrating concern for sustainable development and environmental protection, the governments of the Nordic countries promote universal access to nature and to a high quality of life in the urban milieu. Thus, for example, citizens — children as well as adults — have access to numerous green spaces. Since the 1950s, Sweden has controlled urban sprawl by integrating green spaces within cities, and preserving rural spaces between cities and their suburbs. Swedes of all social classes have access to roads reserved for pedestrians and cyclists, and numerous public facilities assure access to shorelines and bodies of water in which one can swim, even within cities. Moreover, Sweden has ecological neighbourhoods and ecovillages in which housing is accessible. Examples include the neighbourhoods of Björkhagen and Hammarby Sjöstad, near Stockholm, whose residents enjoy high-quality housing, very little automobile traffic, play spaces for children, communal buildings and facilities, as well as numerous green spaces. These neighbourhoods and ecovillages further enlarge the means whereby not just the rich but anybody can access a high-quality environment within the city.

The great availability of public transit allows better access to jobs, schools, and even culture. Moreover, policies contribute to the high usage rate of public transport. The percentage of Stockholm residents who use public transit to get to work during rush hour, 78 percent, is one of the highest in the world. This way of life has several advantages, including some in the domain of public health. Automobile traffic is reduced, along

---

4. Including U.S., Japan, Germany, Australia, Canada, France, U.K., Norway, Austria, Netherlands, Belgium, Switzerland, and Ireland - see http://www.conferenceboard.ca/hcp/details/innovation/publicrandd.aspx.

with car crashes and greenhouse gas emissions; air quality is improved; and people are less sedentary.

Policies aimed at vulnerable populations

Including the homeless

The strategies of the Nordic countries for dealing with homelessness are based on the principle that all citizens should have access to adequate housing, and no-one should be deprived of the right to housing because of dependence on a toxic substance, or problems of mental health or behaviour. What seems to guide the provision of street services as well as financial help is the perspective of empowerment.

According to the Eurocities Working Group on Homelessness, "it is a vital part of Oslo's policy of using its resources efficiently and qualitatively, to accept its responsibility to help every individual to master his own life by regaining control and social skills, for instance in the housing market."[5] The Eurocities working group on homelessness comprised specialists from twelve major European cities, including Copenhagen, Oslo, Stockholm, and Helsinki. They studied homelessness in Europe's 120 largest cities. Sharing their experiences allowed them to conclude as follows: "Homelessness cannot be reduced to housing shortage. Often it has multiple causes and arises from complex individual problems."[6] In this context, it is worthwhile remembering that homelessness can also affect the children of the homeless.

These specialists compiled a list of the best ways of fighting homelessness. According to them, the most effective way is to use strategies that create a "chain of integration" and to adopt a holistic approach. A "chain of integration" is a set of services that support people up to an optimal level of autonomy and integration, according to the following three principles:

1. Professional support of persons at risk means reducing the number of homeless people.
2. The aim of temporary housing should always be the reintegration of persons in autonomous housing.

---

5. Eurocities Working Group on Homelessness. *Cities' Strategies Against Homelessness*, Eurocities, 2006, p. 27.
6. Ibid., p. 4.

Credit: Syldavia, iStock Photo

No one should be deprived of the right to housing because of dependence on drugs, or a problem of mental health or behavior. Copenhagen reserves some of its social housing for itinerants, and many Nordic cities are legally obliged to find housing for all their citizens, including those who are homeless or lack autonomy.

3. The offer of transitional housing accompanied by adapted support (support that varies according to different target groups) encourages the acquisition of skills by most of the homeless, allowing them to become autonomous and to live in their own housing.

The policies in force in the Nordic countries have defined the legal obligations of municipalities for housing, and this constitutes a remarkable achievement. The fight against homelessness is also a concern of municipalities and of social services. Municipalities are required to supply housing to all their citizens, including those who are homeless and those who, because of their age, for example, or a handicap, have special needs. They are also obliged to offer social housing to those excluded from the housing market, those who are nearly insolvent, and those who lack autonomy. Social workers may also establish a personalized plan to respond to particular needs, or set up a permanent scheme.

It is recognized that a multiplicity of ways and means are needed to reduce homelessness: support for hostels, individualized social services, re-insertion apartments, refuges, social housing, etc. To be in a position to offer all these measures, municipalities collaborate with community organizations.

In Denmark, the strategy adopted for fighting homelessness relies on support services that vary with the individual needs of the homeless persons. In Copenhagen, in theory, no one should live on the street because the city is obliged to offer a bed to all its citizens at a maximum cost of 240 euros per month. (As well as having some of the city's social housing reserved for them, the homeless receive about 480 euros per month in welfare.) The city also manages hostels for both short-term (from one day to six months) and long-term stays (from one to three years), and it finances refuges and community hostels. Nonetheless, some people prefer to live on the street and use welfare money for purposes other than rent. Many of them are drug addicts, alcoholics, or mentally ill. In 2006, the number of such persons was estimated to be fifty (the total population of Copenhagen is 580,000).

In Norway, housing allowances are one of the principle tools used to reduce poverty. The government includes them in its policy for fighting homelessness, and plans to increase these allowances and loosen their eligibility criteria. Norwegian social services are responsible for finding temporary lodging for all those who cannot find lodging for themselves. The social services of all municipalities are also obliged to supply lodging to people incapable of meeting their own needs, including those who need adapted housing or need assisted-living and protection services because of age, a handicap, or other reasons.

The empowerment perspective of the policies of the city of Oslo leads to actions intended to facilitate movement along the chain of integration. Thus the city may even go so far as to help renters buy the municipal property they are renting. In the same spirit, one aspect of the national strategy for fighting homelessness includes an economic policy. It focuses on keeping interest rates low and stable so as to reduce the financial risks of the housing market and thus encourage the development of the residential market. One underlying objective of this strategy is to reduce progressively the stock of low-quality temporary housing and maximize the number of citizen-owners. A large proportion of the residents of Oslo (70 percent) now own their own homes.

The city of Oslo also pursues several other goals, including the following: reduce the number of eviction requests by half, and evictions by a third; offer permanent housing to persons recently released from prisons or psychiatric institutions; leave no one in temporary housing for more than three months. Oslo, a city of 648,000 inhabitants, resembles Copenhagen in that it has very few homeless people. At the time of a survey carried out in 2008, its homeless population was 1,500. This number included: people who had no roof under which to spend the night; those who were directed to temporary refuges; prisoners about to be released, and inmates who would be released from institutions within two months; and people living temporarily with friends, acquaintances, or family.

Include the handicapped

The prime objective of policies concerned with the handicapped is to provide technical and human help so as to alleviate the handicap and make such persons as autonomous as possible. The help provided is designed to compensate for the handicap in all aspects of life.

As is the case with gender equity, an integrated approach is taken. This means that including handicapped persons is an obligation that goes beyond the sectors of health and social services. It is an obligation that must be met in an integrated fashion in all public activities and government policies. The underlying principles, as for family and gender equality policies, aim to assure that people have power and influence in their daily lives.

In Sweden, the 2000-2010 national disability action plan shifted perspective. Formerly the focus was on social services, but in the new plan, entitled *From Patient to Citizen*, the accent shifted to the citizen, human rights, and democracy. The objectives: to define obstacles to universal participation, to prevent and combat discrimination, and to promote equality between handicapped boys and girls, and between handicapped women and men.

Legislation establishes rules for protecting handicapped persons from discrimination and for assuring services. In Norway, municipalities are obliged to furnish handicapped people with housing adapted to their needs. In Sweden, the government has passed legislation to assure that the rights of handicapped persons are respected just like those of non-handicapped persons. The legislation includes the Act concerning Support and Service for Persons with Certain Functional Impairments and the Discrimination Act, prohibiting discrimination in the workplace against handicapped persons and unequal treatment for university students, among other things.

Credit: Melker Dahlstrand/imagebank.sweden.se

The proportion of Swedes holding a secondary school diploma is higher amongst the handicapped than in the rest of the population.

An innovative service

In Sweden, the government responded to the demands of handicapped-persons groups by offering, in 1994, something completely new: the service of a personal assistant. Offered with the aim of compensating for the handicap and encouraging the greatest possible autonomy, this service was part of a new policy for developing independence, auto-determination, and full, uncompromised social participation by handicapped persons. Before 1994, such persons had very little voice in their choice of attendants, even in very intimate situations, and had to cope with several different attendants.

The personal assistant service is, in reality, a form of customized support designed to provide a maximum of aid. The handicapped person hires and supervises an assistant in order that the latter may carry out all the tasks the former cannot, whether because of loss of mobility or sight, or intellectual or other deficit. The aid may be provided in a variety of places and situations such as at home, at work, at meetings with friends or family, on holiday, in stores or at the cinema. The spirit of the measure is to limit the number of people who provide services to the handicapped person. Funds are paid directly to the assistant or to the handicapped person. Children and adolescents are entitled to personal assistants at school; in this case, the school authorities hire the assistants. With the exception of those who are deaf or have serious problems of mobility or learning, most handicapped children go to regular schools with other children.

The graduation rate for handicapped persons constitutes an indicator of the success of the Swedish policy. For several years, the proportion of those holding a secondary school diploma has been higher amongst the handicapped than in the rest of the population. In Quebec, in 2006, 33 percent of handicapped persons versus only 22 percent of the non-handicapped population did not have a secondary school diploma.

The role of government organizations

In Sweden, several government organizations play specific roles in facilitating life for handicapped persons. Here are some examples:

1. Samhall is a government body that hires those who cannot find work elsewhere.
2. The Swedish Agency for Participation aims to enable everyone, regardless of their functional abilities, to participate in society, and it favours systematic and effective implementation of disability policy.

Including immigrants

The policies for including immigrants focus first and foremost on access to jobs. "Employment is the optimum road to integration in a new country, for which reason activation activities aimed at this group must be intensified."[7]

---

7. Denmark. Ministry of Socal Affairs, Ministry of Interior Affairs and Health. *National Report on Strategies for Social Protection and Social Inclusion*, 2006. p. 4.

Credit: Ulf Lundkin/imagebank.sweden.se

The Swedish government has set up a program that combines working with learning Swedish. The government pays 75 percent of the salary of persons employed in the private sector and 50 percent of the salary of those in the public sector. Newly arrived immigrants start taking Swedish courses as soon as they arrive and begin looking for work.

Nevertheless, one finds other measures affecting immigrants in the domains of education, gender equity, and citizen participation. For example, measures have been implemented to prevent forced marriages and genital mutilation by organizing information and consciousness-raising sessions on these issues. Forced re-acculturation journeys to countries of origin have also been targeted. The Danish government has released funds to counter such journeys' negative effects on children's school careers and integration. Thus the government provides support to children preparing to leave the country, and to those who return from their country of origin. The inclusion policies also aim to prevent discrimination and the formation of ghettos, and do so particularly by promoting interaction between diverse social groups. The action plans of the Nordic governments concern not only immigrants but also their descendants — that is, children born in Nordic countries to parents born elsewhere.

As the very title of its 2006 "Action plan for the integration and social inclusion of the immigrant population" suggests, the Norwegian government makes a distinction between its integration policy, which deals with the immigrants as soon they arrive, and its longer-term inclusion policy. The aim of the latter is that every person who lives in Norway should be able to participate actively in the society and be equal to all others in the opportunities they can enjoy. The government considers that it is responsible for assuring that immigrants can contribute as quickly as possibly to all aspects of life in society, including professionally. It wishes to prevent the development of a divided society with an immigrant class whose living conditions are worse than those of the rest of the population.

The policy of integration, on the other hand, is aimed at rapidly integrating newly arrived immigrants. The program for welcoming new arrivals, as well as the right, and obligation, to take courses in Norwegian, are among the major measures provided for by this policy. In 2007, the law on learning Norwegian stipulated that municipalities must offer immigrants up to 2,700 hours of instruction in the country's language, as well an obligatory 300 hours of language instruction and Norwegian social studies.

Norwegian measures concerning employment include:

- A programs offering jobs that involve the service of advisors who assure that participants are followed up
- A program for acquiring basic work skills — such as literacy, numeracy, and problem solving — whereby subsidies are given to private enterprises and public agencies that offer such training to their employees, or to the unemployed
- A program, similar to the one for integrating new arrivals, for immigrants who have been living in Norway for several years and who often receive unemployment or welfare benefits
- A total of 250 hours of instruction in Norwegian for those who have applied for refugee status and are awaiting a response.

Particular attention is paid to the adaptation of refugees, as shown by local measures that last for a period of five years after their arrival in the country.

The Norwegian action plan against poverty also includes several measures intended for immigrants, like measures to strengthen their integration into the job market, and measures to promote the inclusion of children and young immigrants.

The Danish government describes its concept of immigrant inclusion in the following words: "Dialogue with ethnic minorities is a key factor. The groups directly affected by Government policies for the area must be consulted and as far as possible included in the democratic decision-making processes. Dialogue is a means of understanding diversity and creating tolerance and cohesion in society."[8]

Two projects focusing on communication with new immigrants follow from this philosophy. The first has the goal of improving dialog with ethnic minorities through activities and meetings with the associations and networks of cultural minorities, such as associations of immigrant women and integration organizations. The second is a project whereby funding is provided for initiatives that promote dialog and understanding between ethnic groups and religions.

The Danish job-access programs are a preferred mode of integration. They include the Versatility program, launched in 2005, which encourages private enterprises to innovate in managing ethnically diverse employees. The program also compiles and communicates the best practices of private companies. To measure the program's effectiveness, the government has quantified objectives for each initiative. It has also formed a coordination group, which includes representatives for all the initiatives implemented. As well, the government has named an external evaluator to evaluate and monitor the program on an ongoing basis.

The Danish government also invests in special projects for dealing with the particular reality of certain immigrants, such as, for example, traumatized refugees. In this spirit, it has decided to finance the Danish Refugee Council for a three-year period to enable the council to set up a knowledge and counselling centre for helping traumatized refugees integrate.

Another specific effort is worthy of mention. The government's action plan to combat men's conjugal violence against women and children comprises activities targeted at immigrant women, since they are more difficult to reach through the regular support services offered to battered women.

---

8. Ibid., p. 27.

Key ideas

*Ensure social inclusion for all and coordination
between political actors*

To ensure that the state would continue investing in social protection and
inclusion even after its mandate had ended, the Danish government of the
day negotiated, in June 2006, a "social protection agreement" with the vari-
ous political parties represented in parliament. The aim of this agreement
is long-term maintenance of the system of social protection.

First, it improves the balance between the number of years in employ-
ment and the number of years in pre-retirement, by gradually (between
2019 and 2022) raising the age of pre-retirement to 62, and (between 2024
and 2027) raising the retirement age from 65 to 67. These thresholds will
be adjusted as a function of the life expectancy of a 60-year-old so as to
ensure an anticipated retirement period lasting 19.5 years.

Secondly, the government proposes measures to increase the employ-
ment of persons with health or social problems, paying particular attention
to immigrants. By raising the retirement age, and by deploying immi-
grant-integration and education measures, it anticipates creating jobs for
110,000 additional persons by 2025, and for 125,000 more by 2050. In the
same vein, the government aims to make Denmark one of the world's
leading knowledge-centric societies.

Thirdly, the agreement between the political parties allows the govern-
ment to allocate its socio-economic resources in anticipation of the long-
term future, with the aim of maintaining social cohesion and avoiding an
increase in socio-economic disparity. It plans to create a healthy society
and avoid divisions between the well-off and the poor.

Help the homeless

Stockholm launched its "roof-over-the head guarantee" in 1999. This muni-
cipal service for the homeless guarantees a place to sleep for those who do
not have one. The services must meet quantified objectives. Anyone can
use the service, with the exception of the few homeless people who are
violent or threatening.

The city's social services office has created a register of beds available
in refuges and other types of housing, whether in the community, govern-
mental, or private sectors. The coordinator of the register regularly meets

with the various refuges to learn of changes in the clientele and new needs. The register records how each person lodged was transported to the refuge, and the number of times the person had recourse to it. An evaluation of this service concluded that its guarantee of a roof for the night was indeed honoured. There are an estimated 3,000 people with no fixed address in Stockholm, of whom 500 are likely to sleep outdoors. Those who fight against homelessness are not all in agreement about this measure. Some would prefer that the state invest in long-term solutions rather than in sporadic fixes. All, however, agree that the two types of measures are needed.

Reach out to the homeless in the street

Copenhagen has set up teams of street workers based in each of the city's fifteen social service centres. The mission of these professionals is to prevent repeated episodes of homelessness by providing help adapted to the needs of the homeless.

The city has also created four street dispensaries in each of which a doctor and nurses look after homeless persons who do not use regular healthcare services.

Control the low-grade housing market

Many people lived in rooming houses in Oslo in the 1990s. Since demand exceeded supply, landlords could easily ask high rents for poor-quality rooms. To correct this situation, the city raised the housing-quality standards, and took other measures to reduce demand. Use of such private hostels must now be limited in time and based on quality agreement contracts. Since then, recourse to such lodging has decreased by 90 percent and, according to the Eurocities Working Group on Homelessness, the city "now has a fairly good control of the situation in that part of the housing market."[9]

Implement effective projects with immigrants

In a small Copenhagen suburb, Job Express, a project helping those looking for work, was launched in underprivileged neighbourhoods in which

9. Eurocities Working Group on Homelessness. *Cities' Strategies Against Homelessnesss*, Eurocities, 2006, p. 28.

numerous immigrants live. This project, which used innovative methods, had unhoped-for success. Within two years, more than 250 people had found a job and 30 young people obtained a training period. The project contributed to modify the city's employment policy, and its approaches were integrated in social and employment public services. Personalized accompanying measures as well as the idea of coordinated and rapid interventions were generalized and are now adopted by other Denmark municipalities.

The close contacts established between local partners — such as the businesses and social housing agencies — who, before the project began, rarely communicated, help explain the success of this initiative. Other factors in its success include:

- Setting up the project at the local level.
- The immigrant status of many of the agents helping people find work.
- The accent placed on speed, that is, on the need to find a job quickly.
- The insistence on actively seeking work rather than on justifying failures.
- The drawing up of job applications on the first day of participation in the project.
- The close collaboration with the social housing sector, the business community, and the local government.

Combine work and language learning

To increase the chances of finding work for those who have just arrived in the country, Sweden has set up a program of social inclusion which combines work with learning the Swedish language. Thus the government contributes 75 percent of the salary of employees in the private sector, and 50 percent for those in the public service. The aim of the program is that newly arrived persons take courses in Swedish as soon as they arrive and that they rapidly find work. These courses are offered as soon as the process of looking for work begins.

Reach parents through their children

Norway has implemented measures aimed at improving Norwegian among young children before they go to school. Several of these measures include a component targeting parents in order to improve their linguistic competence. Hourly slots in daycares are offered free to immigrant children who do not yet attend daycare, and there is follow-up of parents and caregivers at home, to monitor how their Norwegian is improving. The language skills of children of pre-school age are monitored in public-health centres so that the children can be well prepared for school. As well, parents who are learning the language are monitored. Moreover, the National Center for Multicultural Education at the Oslo University College, in collaboration with the Norwegian Directorate for Education and Training, is carrying out a pilot study on the learning of Norwegian by families, and on the teaching of the language in daycares, as children make the transition from daycare to primary school, and then to secondary school. Another project consists of helping parents encourage their children to read in Norwegian at home by distributing a tool, designed for them and translated into several languages, entitled *Make space for reading at home.*

Compensate for the deficiencies of previous education

In Norway a program aims to increase the number of young immigrants who earn a College/CEGEP-level diploma. The program is based on evaluations carried out by the National Center for Multicultural Education at Oslo University College in order to assure that the offer is well adapted to the reality of young immigrants. Operating in adult-education and college-level establishments, this program targets young people who have only recently arrived in Norway and have little education. The program draws on secondary-school teachers. Hiring bilingual teachers as advisers allows better communication with the young immigrants and their parents about the college and career choices.

The government has also mandated the National Center for Multicultural Education, in conjunction with the Norwegian Directorate for Education and Training, to design tests for children and youth. The goal: to evaluate their level of literacy in their maternal language, their linguistic competencies, and the level of instruction they have received in their country of origin.

CHAPTER 10

Sustainable Development at the Local Level

This chapter tackles sustainable development at the local level and high-lights some projects undertaken under municipal mandates. We have limited our study to the Nordic capitals — Stockholm, Copenhagen, Oslo, and Helsinki — so as to have examples that can be transposed to urban realities. In the context of sustainable development, the Nordic model applies to cities for it is significantly based on the decentralization of power to cities. Cities raise relatively high taxes and exercise a very wide range of responsibilities.

First, to clearly delineate the Scandinavian model, we will present the principles that characterize sustainable development in the Nordic capitals, as well as some national programs. Secondly, to illustrate concretely the Nordic way of designing a sustainable-development strategy, we will give an overview of Stockholm's 2008-2011 environmental plan. Held up as an example of good practice in environmental management and planning by the European Union, this plan is at the heart of the city's sustainable development activities.

The Nordic model of sustainable development

Involvement of the state and national laws

Nordic cities develop in a context favourable to designing and imple-menting sustainable development programs thanks to government involve-ment and national legislation. An example comes from the top: in 2008, the prime ministers of each of the Nordic countries signed the Declaration on a Sustainable Nordic Region, affirming the importance of sustainable development and of counteracting climate change. Moreover, they defined state involvement, notably in issues of social protection, as a condition of sustainable development:

> Sustainable development is about meeting the needs of the current generation without jeopardizing the ability of future generations to satisfy their needs. We need to improve welfare provision and the quality of life for current and future generations, and preserve the Earth's ability to sustain life in all its diversity.[1]

This Declaration sets out the relationship between the actions of the state and the underlying principles of sustainable development, namely: "democracy, the rule of law and respect for fundamental rights, including freedom, gender equality and equal opportunities for all."[2]

Moreover, the national governments pass laws that establish a context helpful for the cities. In 2006, for example, the Swedish government passed a law obliging the big gasoline dealers to sell renewable fuels as well. In 2011, this obligation was extended to small gas dealers. Stockholm has set itself the goal of ending its dependence on fossil fuels between now and 2050. Not only is the Swedish law consistent with the city's ambitious goal, but in establishing high standards and encouraging daring decisions, the law also breaks the path for other levels of government. The repercussions are indisputable.

Sustainable Communities in Europe: A Cross-National Assessment of the Implementation of Agenda 21 at the Local Level of Governance reports on a study evaluating the local-level implementations in several European countries of initiatives taken as part of the UN's sustainable development action plan for the twenty-first century, known as Agenda 21. The study found a clear correlation between, on the one hand, the importance of the Agenda 21 initiatives taken by a country's cities, and on the other, the importance of the support provided by the national government and the integration of the Agenda 21 plan in national policies.

The authors of this study stressed that, mainly because of its influence on how resources are allocated, the constitutional structure of a state (federal or unitary) seems to play a role in the local-level implementation of Agenda 21 initiatives. Because in unitary states — such as the Nordic countries — central and local governments are better integrated and have more

---

1. Nordic Council of Ministers. *Sustainable Development–New Bearings for the Nordic Countries*, Copenhagen, Revised edition, 2009, p. 5.
2. Ibid., p. 5.

Credit: Howard Stenzel

All urban development in Oslo is designed to densify the city so as to protect green spaces, which are very important in the eyes of residents. Such spaces cover 20 percent of the city area (11 percent in Montreal), and 94 percent of Osloites live within 300 meters of a green space. There is a consensus favouring preservation of the forests and lakes surrounding Oslo over urban development, so as to offer citizens a unique lifestyle, with almost instant access to wilderness.

flexible relationships than in federated states, implementation of national policies at the local level seems to be more effective. Federated states, in contrast, are more rigid in defining the scope of their responsibility and more jealous in defending it; and any added responsibility can give rise to epic debates on areas of responsibility.

A holistic vision

The starting point for the development of public policy in Nordic countries and cities is often a holistic vision that encompasses more than just the issue the policy itself addresses. This vision allows the issue to be seen in relation to external factors which, in turn, provide interveners with a better grasp of what the policy can and should do for society.

Credit: Ola Ericson/imagebank.sweden.se

In the 1990, Stockholm began converting Hammarby Sjöstad, an old and decrepit port zone, into a residential neighborhood that conforms to sustainable development standards. The Hammarby model has become a benchmark in the management of energy, solid wastes, and waste water. Most of the energy that residents consume is solar or wind energy, or comes from biogas produced by treating waste waters. Though the neighborhood is near the center of the city, each of its buildings has both street and park frontage. Residents can swim in Lack Sikla, which borders the neighbourhood. Recycling bins integrated into the landscape serve to collect recyclable wastes, which are then automatically conveyed by a suction system through an underground network to a treatment center.

The common good

For example, the common declaration of the Nordic countries on sustainable development articulates a global vision that explicitly comprises not only the usual three dimensions of sustainable development (economic, social, and ecological), but also goals to be reached in sub-dimensions with extended ramification: a high level of education and training, full employment, solidarity, social and territorial cohesion, a safe and peaceful world, good public health, etc.

The Nordic model is based on recognition of the interdependence of such sub-dimensions and an uncompromising focus on the common good. Public health, for example, is considered both a prerequisite for and consequence of reaching sustainable development goals, as indicated by this passage from a document on sustainable development by the Nordic Council of Ministers:

> Economic growth is important to sustainable development because the resources it generates can be invested in social development and measures to improve the environment. Growth must not cause irreversible damage to the environment and the renewable capacity of natural resources, nor can it be at the expense of people's health and well-being, which are, in turn, also preconditions for economic growth.[3]

The city of Oslo's green space strategy is a good example of the global vision transposed to the municipal level. Because it includes the social, cultural, environmental, and material dimensions of accessibility to green and natural spaces, European experts who have evaluated this strategy characterize its approach as 'holistic'. Oslo compares a city to a cultural biotope (a specific biological milieu offering a stable habitat for a group of animal and vegetable species), which integrates human habitat and biological diversity, as well as natural cycles that work well.

A noteworthy fact, indicating once again the holistic conception of governmental interventions, is that the Swedish and Finnish organizations responsible for applying housing policies belong to the Environment Ministries. This is logical, for their policies are linked to urban and rural development, and also affect habitat in the larger sense of the term.

Moreover, the city of Oslo's sustainable development strategy illustrates global — that is, planet-wide — concerns. The following extract demonstrates a certain cultural gap between Quebec and the Nordic countries; few municipalities in Quebec would dare make such statements and propose such noble goals:

> We stand at a critical moment in Earth's history, a time when humanity must choose its future. As the world becomes increasingly interdependent and fragile, the future at once holds great peril and great promise. To move forward we must recognize that in the midst of a magnificent diversity of cultures and life forms we are one human family and one Earth community with a common destiny. We must join together to bring forth a sustainable global society founded on respect for nature, universal human rights,

3. Nordic Council of Ministers. *Sustainable Development—New Bearings for the Nordic Countries*, Copenhagen, revised edition 2009, p. 7.

Credit: City of Oslo

Oslo has measured noise levels at various points in its territory and drawn up a map that informs residents of the spatial distribution of noise. The city strives to preserve some quiet spaces throughout its territory, and to ensure that everyone has access to these spaces.

economic justice, and a culture of peace. Towards this end, it is imperative that we, the peoples of Earth, declare our responsibility to one another, to the greater community of life, and to future generations.[4]

The economy

Economic growth is treated in the same uncompromising philosophy and with the same holistic perspective. Whatever the issue — equality between men and women, say, or social inclusion — the Nordic countries and cities advocate a global, long-term vision, one in which the economic dimension occupies a central place. It is no surprise, therefore, that the economy should be taken into account in sustainable development. According to the Nordic Council of Ministers, "economic growth is a prerequisite for a sustainable society, and a sustainable society is the only way to long-term economic growth."[5]

---

4. Oslo. *Strategy for Sustainable Development: Environment and Sustainability Status 2002, Urban Ecology Programme 2002-2014*, 2002, p. 41.
5. Council of Ministers. *Sustainable Development–New Bearings for the Nordic Countries*, Copenhagen, 2009, p. 5.

Credit: Gitte Lotinga

Numerous Copenhageners get around using cargo tricycles equipped with a box in front which can even carry adults. It is not unusual to see two children in the cargo box. In fact, 25 percent of families with two or more children own a cargo tricycle, and 50 percent of Copenhageners who do own one use it to transport their children. The cargo box also serves for transporting heavy objects. To see an entertaining video on how Copenhageners use their cargo bikes: http://www.youtube.com/watch?v=voSEpVo33AM.

Stockholm's environmental program clearly situates economic growth in these terms: "There is no conflict between sustainable growth and modern environmental thinking. Environmental work must take place throughout the entire community, bringing together businesses, individuals, organizations and public agencies."[6]

Oslo's sustainable development strategy also unequivocally insists on the importance of having a vigorous economy. It reminds readers that if a city is poor, it cannot offer its residents decent living conditions or a high-quality environment, because it cannot invest in these sectors. On the other hand, if a city does not offer a healthy environment and the

---

6. Stockholm. *The Stockholm Environment Programme 2008-2011–Overarching goals and priorities*, 2008, p. 2.

possibility of wealth creation, it is less attractive than other cities to brains and businesses.

Copenhagen designates the environment as a lever of economic growth, and is home to a number of enterprises developing clean technologies. In partnership with neighbouring cities and several businesses and research institutes, Copenhagen has set up an innovation park dedicated to eco-friendly projects, with the goal of turning the Danish capital region into a knowledge hub. Some 37 cities, institutions, and firms participate in this project, and by developing instruments, models, courses, and tests, they aim at strengthening innovation, competences and knowledge sharing in renovation projects that use green energy. The goal of the initiative is to position the region and Denmark advantageously on the international scene in the realm of green construction.

Moreover, Copenhagen created the Copenhagen Cleantech Cluster in 2009, to facilitate access to the city's entire clean technology sector. Its mission was to promote growth, competitiveness, and innovation in clean technology and to facilitate cooperation at the international scale (Denmark is one of the world's largest exporters of such technology). The financing ended in 2014 but the organization merged with Lean Energy Cluster to become CLEAN and facilitate business, highlight investment opportunities, offers seminars, etc. Clean Edge, an influential American research and advisory firm, has classed the Copenhagen initiative as one of the ten most important clean technology clusters in the world. The Copenhagen Cleantech Cluster had a budget of $30 million for five years provided by various levels of government (the capital region, the Zealand region, and the European Union.) The new cluster now has 161 members, including major firms in the sector, the University of Copenhagen, linked cities, and an industrial confederation. It aims to create jobs and public-private partnerships, and to establish collaborations with international clean technology clusters. Successful companies already involved include Stirling DK, PhotoSolar, EcoXpac, and Better Place Denmark.

Health

The global perspective adopted by the Nordic countries is such that questions of health are naturally included in the environmental or sustainable development strategies of the Nordic capitals.

Stockholm's environmental program is designed by its environment department, officially known as the Environment and Health Administration. The program is developed considering not only the environmental situation, but also the health risks of the status quo. A portrait of public health risks is drawn up for each sector of activity. Risks are presented for sectors including transport (notably, ozone produced by nitrogen oxide and hydrocarbons), energy (the finger of blame was pointed at wood stoves), water (cleanliness, access to nature and to bodies of water), and waste management (in particular, the question of dangerous waste was raised).

Oslo's sustainable development strategy well integrates the social aspects of health and describes the challenges facing the city, which include, notably, an increase in unhealthy lifestyles, an aging population, and growth in immigration.

In Copenhagen, 60 percent of the population lived less than fifteen minutes by foot from a green space (park or natural area) or a blue space (beach or sea swimming pool, for instance) in 2007. The objective for 2015 was to increase this to 90 percent. The city unreservedly endorses the claim that "Research has shown that … green and blue areas can contribute decisively to city-dwellers' health and wellbeing."[7] Several new parks have been developed and at the beginning of 2015, 80 percent of Copenhageners lived within 300 meters of a park.

The role of government and the decentralization of power

A characteristic feature of Nordic countries and cities is the strong presence of the state, acting as a counterweight to the free market. The state invests and intervenes, creating programs or adapting regulations that can modulate the activities of the free market according to the goals of sustainable development. Decentralization to local and regional levels is another characteristic of political power in the Nordic countries.

A tradition of intervention

Nordic governments, both at the national and local levels, resolutely intervene to attenuate the environmental impacts of human activities.

At the national level, parliaments do not hesitate to legislate so as to assure the common good in several spheres of life. Their interventions are desired and welcomed by the population. In all the Nordic countries,

---

7. Copenhagen. *Eco-Metropolis–Our Vision for Copenhagen 2015*, Technical and Environmental Administration, 2007, p. 15.

socio-democratic parties or coalitions have held power for several decades and all these parties on the left have advocated such a role for the state. For instance, the Swedish socio-democratic model prevailed in managing the country's Agenda 21 initiatives: the national authorities rapidly took charge of guiding the whole process and supported the initiatives so that they were both economically and socially profitable.

At the local level, the cities propose regulations and projects to assure that development is sustainable. Both within municipal management and explicitly in programs for citizens, suggestions and initiatives are proposed that further sustainable development goals, such as, for example, support for the purchase of eco-friendly cars, creation of green neighbourhoods, eco-energetic construction, and revitalization projects. In terms of internal management, it is the city councils, whose members are elected, who take responsibility for municipal sustainable development programs. In Stockholm, the objectives of the city's environmental program become those of the city council right away.

The following example indicates the range of the powers of intervention of a typical city. In partnership with the industrial sector (and with the help of funding from the European Union, among other sources) Stockholm launched a whole series of measures to oblige gas stations to sell alternative fuel and encourage car dealers to sell vehicles that run on such fuel.

The city began by financially supporting one oil company and thus convincing it to offer alternative fuel. It then helped the private sector coordinate efforts to buy eco-friendly cars in bulk at reasonable prices, and to offer new models on the market. It also encouraged the production of its own biogas and established a distribution system capable of meeting present and future needs. It set up local incentive measures, such as free parking and, through talks with the Swedish government and in collaboration with other cities and NGOs, contributed to national-level incentive measures. The national government then agreed to offer tax credits to owners of eco-friendly vehicles, first on a trial basis, and then as a long-term measure. For its part, the city of Stockholm subsidized the acquisition of four models of eco-friendly cars and bought several vehicles for its municipal fleet, so as to test them before choosing which ones to promote. Concurrently a marketing campaign targeted mainly at journalists was launched. They were given the opportunity to use such vehicles, with the explicit goal of making the population aware of the importance of eco-friendly vehicles. The same test-drive opportunity was offered to small companies which a study had identified as having environmental profiles making them likely to buy such vehicles.

Today, the percentage of eco-friendly vehicles in Stockholm is one of the highest in Europe. In 2012, 50 percent of car sales in Stockholm were of eco-friendly vehicles. Moreover, 98 precent of the city's own vehicles are green. The estimated result is a reduction in carbon dioxide emissions of more than 100,000 tons per year. Some challenge the choice of including in the list of vehicles eligible for the national government's fiscal exemption vehicles that, though their carbon dioxide emissions are below certain limits, still burn diesel or gasoline, yet it remains true that no fewer than 75 percent of the vehicles for which such eco-friendly exemptions are claimed burn neither diesel nor gasoline, but run on ethanol, biogas, natural gas, or electricity.

Marked decentralization and extended fields of responsibility

In the Nordic countries, governmental authorities that encourage social development through social services, education, or welfare, belong to the municipal level and are directly administered by cities. In addition, cities manage primary and secondary schools, as well as daycare centres. Moreover, in three of the countries studied — Sweden, Norway, and Finland — health services are run by regional or local authorities. These enjoy significant taxing power (the bulk of health and medical costs in Sweden are paid for by county council and municipal taxes). According to the extent of local needs, the national government also allocates financial resources. Cities make the majority of public expenditures.

These arrangements, of course, give cities, in partnership with the organizations they manage, a relatively large degree of freedom of action in applying the principles of sustainable development. In Copenhagen, a large number of public daycares and kindergartens have reached the city's goal: 90 percent of the food they buy is organic. In other city organizations, 50 percent of the food offered in various kitchens and cafeterias is organic. These successes were not won by supplementary funding; rather, they were due to improvements in the knowledge of kitchen staff, to the transmission of information and advice, and to acquiring new recipes and new ways of doing things.

So, the question that can be asked is: does the fact that cities manage social assistance services and are close to the regional authorities that manage health services make them aware of the importance of creating programs that encourage health and social inclusion? This probably explains the frequent integration of health questions in environmental strategies. Thus Stockholm's environmental program directly and explicitly tackles "key environmental issues and health risks."[8]

Lafferty and Coenen (2000) have pointed out the fact that implementing the Agenda 21 initiatives has been easier in the Nordic countries where cities enjoy greater decision-making autonomy than in other European countries where other models of governance prevail. Moreover, it is interesting to note that the Nordic model of decentralized government is reproduced in Stockholm's environmental program. This model means that national ministries design the policies and the main lines to be followed, while implementation, the detailed development of strategies, the provision of services and administration are decentralized, to become the responsibility of regional or municipal agencies. The city of Stockholm's environment program works in a similar way. The city established the major goals, leaving to the various administrative sub-units the task of choosing actions to meet these goals.

The integrated and systematic approach

Governments now adopt the integrated approach in designing and implementing policies. This means that policies are multi-sectoral, with principles which must be integrated with those of all ministries and agencies. The policies of gender equity and those concerning handicapped persons are examples of such multi-sectoral policies.

The integrated approach is also widely used in sustainable development strategies. These are designed to affect all stakeholders and guide all municipal administrative units following a global vision of desired results. In Oslo, for example, the policy of sustainability is reflected in regulations governing municipal purchasing. The action plans that follow from Stockholm's environmental program, such as action plans on climate change, on water management, and on waste management, serve as a basis for developing the city's budget. Local plans are also interwoven into regional and national plans. Helsinki's services and agencies include environmental management in their management services. Moreover, the implementation of the sustainable development plan is integrated along with the urban development orientation in the central administration's planning system.

---

8. Stockholm. *The Stockholm Environment Programme 2008-2011—Overarching goals and priorities*, 2008, p. 2.

The integrated approach is favoured by systematized processes for implementing plans and policies, especially the use of environmental management systems, systematic evaluations and integrated follow-up.

Various municipal administrations are certified in the use of environmental management systems (EMS). In Oslo, 291 of the city's 800 administrative units and municipal agencies (including those in education and health) have certified environmental management systems, and thirteen of them are certified according to ISO 14001 standards. In Copenhagen, six of the seven administrations of the City of have received the latter certification. This means that two-thirds of the employees of the City (Denmark's largest enterprise) work in units that are certified.

Stockholm has launched an online tool for the everyday management of its various services. This tool must be used for planning operations, thus integrating activities generated by the city's environmental program and facilitating integration of its objectives in current activities. Environmental issues affect all aspect of management: operations planning, budgets, evaluations, and follow-up.

Evaluations and scientific data

It is the custom in the Nordic countries to base political decisions on scientific data and to resort to studies in order to clearly delineate what is at stake before designing policies or making plans. Moreover, these countries are quite systematic in their use of evaluations, either to measure progress towards long-term goals, or to assess the results of policies or programs. Sustainable development at the local level is no exception. As the city of Stockholm reports, regarding its action program against greenhouse gas emissions:

> Targets for the Action Programme are outlined based on an assessment (of current level of emissions) and a prognosis (of future levels of emissions in a business-as-usual scenario). This forms the foundation of a programme or plan for collective strategies and measures. At the end of the programme, when the measures have been implemented, a follow-up of the process and results is carried out.[9]

Thus Stockholm's environmental program is systematically evaluated. For example, the city has produced several evaluation reports just in the domain of climate change, with titles such as "Adapting to climate change

---

9. City of Stockholm. *Stockholm's Action Programme Against Greenhouse Gas Emissions,* 2008.

in Stockholm," "Effects of climate change on polluted land," "Effects from climate change on biodiversity," and "Report on carbon dioxide emissions in the city of Stockholm."

In 2001, Copenhagen distributed 4,500 questionnaires in the form of postcards to cyclists in the city. Of these, fifteen percent were returned. This led to those bike path sections in need of improvement being identified. In 2011, the city improved all sections that five or more cyclists had identified in the survey as needing work.

In 2007, Copenhagen adopted a plan to turn the city into an eco-metropolis. Evaluations were carried out in various domains such as active transport (in particular, bicycles), road safety for cyclists, carbon dioxide emissions, the proximity and use of green and blue (such as pools) spaces, the consumption of organic food, or the cleanliness of streets. In 2014, Copenhagen earned the title of European Green Capital of the year by the European Commission.

Collaboration and participative democracy

Collaboration and consensus decision-making are the preferred ways of doing things in Nordic political culture. When a decision is made, the tradition is to try to reach a consensus position, one to which all government partners, such as citizens' groups and businesses, can stick.

The Climate Pact, signed in 2007 by the city of Stockholm and several of the businesses active in the region, is an example of a sustainable development initiative based on collaboration. The pact aims to get the city and the business sector to unite in their efforts to reduce negative climate effects on the residents, workers, and businesses of the municipality of Stockholm. The list of signatories is impressive; it includes some 50 municipal agencies and 179 companies such as Shell, Taxi Stockholm, and Electrolux. Their global objective is to reduce their emissions or reach certain targets set by the Stockholm environmental program. Each year, a report summarizing the progress of each of the signatories is published. This report publicizes businesses' 'clean' achievements and stimulates improvements. The pact also serves as a forum in which participants can exchange their know-how and experience.

The authorities running Nordic cities put the democratic process at the heart of their activities. Citizens are consulted on many subjects — on real estate developments, for example — and their suggestions have real influence on the projects. Thus programs for fixing up old or disadvan-

Credit: Copenhagenize Consulting

Copenhagen wants to be a cycling capital. Traffic lights on the main road are synchronized as function of the speed of cyclists rather than that of drivers. Moreover, a first bike highway has been designed to facilitate long-distance journeys between suburbs and the city centre. Its wide lanes, smooth surface, and traffic-light synchronization allow cyclists to ride rapidly and with few stops. Twenty-one local governments collaborated to create this Cycle Super Highway. In 2012, 36 percent of the total number of people working or studying in Copenhagen cycled to their place of work or education, and the city wanted to increase this percentage to 50 percent by the end of 2015. In May 2015, 45 percent did. If we count only residents of Copenhagen, this percentage rises to 63 percent. Some employers contribute by making available waterproof ponchos that their employees can borrow in case of rain.

taged neighbourhoods in Copenhagen rely, at every stage of the projects, on residents' suggestions and participation. Following their suggestions, projects include, for example, developing community centres, re-greening plots of land, or adding bike supports.

While on this subject, it should be noted that the culture of democratic involvement is also reflected in the high rates of participation in municipal elections. Between 2001 and 2008, the participation rate in elections in the Nordic capitals peaked at 85 percent of voters, and was usually between 70 and 80 percent. The voter turnout for the 2010 Stockholm municipal elections was 82 percent. It should also be pointed out that municipal elections are combined with national elections and take place on fixed dates, and

Credit: Copenhagenize Consulting

In Copenhagen, it is municipal policy to prioritize bike path maintenance, which is done using small vehicles. Road maintenance comes second. To clearly mark the bike paths, they are raised some 10 to 15 cm above the street (while still being lower than the sidewalks).

that proportional representation used by the electoral system fosters strong participation.

Financial investments

The Nordic capitals invest large sums in sustainable development programs. Their goal is to improve the health and well-being of people and, either by preventing or fixing damage, to protect the environment. These generous programs are seen as investments with returns, in several domains, that are reckoned to be very good. As in the case of social programs, sustainable development investments reflect the philosophy of high standards that characterizes the Nordic model — and that, despite globalization, remains intact. Here are several concrete illustrations of this philosophy.

Stockholm will invest 150 million euros over a period of fifteen years in programs related to bicycle use: improvement and expansion of the bike-path network, traffic lights, dedicated bike parking, etc. The city also worked with funding from the Environmental Billion Fund, a fund made available through the sale of the energy company previously owned by the City. From 2004 to 2010, 120 million euros were granted to finance 158 projects under municipal administration and companies.

The budget forecast for developing collective transport in the Oslo region for the period from 2008 to 2028 amounts to CAN$9 billion, of which 80 percent will come from collective transport revenues and highway tolls, and 20 percent from the national government. The money will serve to develop infrastructure and improve various aspects of service, including punctuality, frequency, comfort, the condition of stations, and the number of vehicles.

Wide dissemination of information

The Nordic cities base their policies and programs on scientific results. Moreover, they are committed to spreading scientific data and knowledge widely so as to communicate the facts on which they ground their policies.

Thus municipal documents cite many studies. Copenhagen's bicycle transportation policy, for example, reports a multitude of data including the results of a study on how safe cyclists feel in the city: 57 percent do feel safe (and it is hoped that this percentage will rise to 80 percent), and 24 percent feel somewhat safe. The report also cites the number of collisions involving bicycles, the proportion of cyclists aged forty and over, and the proportion of all trips that were made by bike. The report also includes tables and graphics showing how these data have changed over the years.

A guide that Oslo's Department of Environmental Affairs and Transport produced on the reduction of greenhouse gas emissions includes such data as the following: converting 13 percent of the 27,000 oil-fired heating systems in the Oslo region to burn biofuel would reduce GHG emissions by 300,000 tons per year.

Finally, Stockholm's environmental program includes a host of statistics confirming the state of affairs on which, in turn, the program's objectives are based. Let us cite just the following passage, drawn from the chapter on environmentally efficient transport: "Of particulate matter in Stockholm, 67 percent comes from transport, primarily from light vehicles. Levels in Stockholm in 2006 varied between 13 and 38 µg/m³ as an annual average at the five monitoring sites in Stockholm."[10] A table showing the changes in these data from 1994 to 2006 completed the communication process.

---

10. Stockholm. *The Stockholm Environment Programme 2008-2011–Overarching goals and priorities*, 2008, p. 14.

The strategies of the Nordic capitals

The Nordic capitals have produced several plans and programs to take action locally on sustainable development, the environment, and climate change issues. As well, each of the capitals has an Agenda 21 action plan, usually focused on neighbourhood projects and on strengthening links between citizens and the administration.

The European Union cites Stockholm's Environmental Plan 2008-2011 as an example of good practice in environmental management and planning. This document, central to the city's sustainable development strategy, typifies the detailed plans drawn up by the Nordic capitals.

Environmental accomplishments

The achievements of Stockholm, the city named European Green Capital by the European Commission in 2010, are numerous. After comparing 35 European cities on ten dimensions of environmental action, committees of experts judged Stockholm to be the most praiseworthy. Many successful projects bear witness to Stockholm's effort at sustainable development. Here are two examples.

First, mass transit. Investments in public transit have contributed to a constant decline in rush-hour car use since 1988, with the percentage of journeys made by car between 6 and 9 a.m. dropping from 81 to 59 percent. In parallel, the proportion of people using mass transit rose in ten years from 57 to 64 percent. The number of cyclists also rose. The proportion of all those going to work at rush hour who use mass transit (78 percent) is one of the highest in the world.

Secondly, the reduction in GHG emissions. Numerous programs for reducing GHG emissions in Stockholm have succeeded in reducing per capita emissions by 25 percent since 1990. Making alternative fuels available at the city's gas stations was one of the initiatives that contributed to this result. Today, more than 85 percent of Stockholm's gas stations offer such fuels.

Stockholm's strategy: the city's environmental program

Stockholm's environmental program serves as a global environmental policy, and includes sections dealing with sustainable development. The program is a kind of master plan: it states global objectives, while sec-

Credit: Melker Dahlstrand/imagebank.sweden.se

At rush hour, 78 percent of Stockholmers get to work using public transit (compared to only 28.5 percent of Montrealers). The importance of the car compared to all other means of transport has been steadily declining since 1998.

toral plans set specific objectives and define actions to be taken. Thus the environmental program is of central importance to Stockholm's sustainable development.

The 2008-2011 Stockholm Environment Program presents itself as a pan-municipal policy. It deals with six themes or sectors of activity that are considered to have priority:

1. Environmentally efficient transport
2. Goods and buildings free of dangerous substances
3. Sustainable use of energy
4. Sustainable use of land and water
5. Waste treatment with minimal environmental impact
6. A healthy indoor environment.

As pointed out above, the program states the main objectives to be reached in each of the above-mentioned sectors, but does not impose specific actions. Rather, in various domains (GHGs, energy, wastes, etc.), the city proposes action plans which include concrete measures and sectoral objectives,

Credit: Ola Ericson/imagebank.sweden.se

Stockholm is an archipelago. The fact that there are only 18 points of entry to the city facilitated setting up a toll system and reducing its costs relative to those of the system in London, which has 200 points of entry. Montreal, being an island, is like Stockholm in having only a small number — 19 — of entry points. The toll system in Stockholm was twinned with an increase in the supply of public transport and of incentive parking places, a massive information campaign, and a set of evaluations (social benefits and costs, impacts on the economy, health, and traffic). After trying the system for seven months, a 20 percent reduction in traffic and revenue of $11 million in tolls were recorded. All these sums are re-invested in public transport.

and complement the environmental program. There are several such plans, and they have produced several reports. Here are some examples:

- Action programs on Climate Change (1995-2000 and 2000-2005)
- Follow-up report on the program on climate change 2000-2005
- Plan for reducing greenhouse gas emissions between now and 2015
- Municipal energy plan
- Evaluation report on adaptation to climate change in Stockholm
- Evaluation report on the effects of climate change on terrestrial pollution
- Evaluation report on the effects of climate change on biodiversity.

Program objectives

The program defines the goals to be reached in each of the sectors. For example, in the transport sector, the city's fleet must consist entirely of 'green' cars, and 85 percent of the fuel they use must come from renewable resources. In the energy sector, the goal is to reduce energy consumption by 10 percent during the program period (2008-2011). And a goal under the theme 'goods and buildings free of dangerous substances,' is that at least 15 percent of the food the city purchases should be organic.

The program distinguishes between two types of objectives: those that can be reached directly by the municipal administration, and those on which the city can only act indirectly, by supporting other stakeholders. For example, the section on the theme of goods and buildings free of dangerous substances states that since the use of cadmium is already regulated by law, all that municipal authorities can do is to inform the population of how important it is to reduce contamination by this metal.

Statistics and scientific foundations

For each of the six general objectives, the program summarizes the current situation and the challenges to be met. It also mentions the harmful consequences that inaction would have on public health and the environment. The program describes the problems, the trends towards improvement or deterioration, the factors at play, and what the city is able to do to improve the situation. All is thoroughly summarized; all is clear and easy to understand.

Exhaustive analyses of the factors acting on the environment and on health allow inclusion in the program of overviews, well supported by statistics, of the situation for each of the target goals. For example, in treating the goal of environmentally efficient transport, the program indicates that transport and industrial machinery generate three-quarters of Stockholm's carbon dioxide emissions. As well, the program points out that shipping goods contributes a small share of Stockholm's air pollution: six percent of the city's nitrogen oxide emissions, and two percent of its sulfur oxide emissions.

Implementation by the stakeholders

Moreover, the program specifies which municipal administrative units are associated with each of the six general objectives, and which have the

Credit: Cecilia Larsson/imagebank.sweden.se

Recycling is part of the Swedish culture. It is not unusual to see Swedes bring various objects to the recycling stations. All sales of beverages in plastic bottles or metal cans is prohibited unless there is an approved system for recycling the containers. In 2009, 77 percent of all packaging and newspapers were recycled.

responsibility of evaluating the results of efforts to reach these targets. In each unit, the key stakeholders are designated. Their support is indispensable, as is adapting the objectives to the realities of how the city works.

The professionals in the municipal administrative units must themselves determine which measures are pertinent, and choose to implement the most cost-effective of these measures. This task includes choosing, in collaboration with the city's executive committee, indicators for measuring how well global objectives have been reached.

Each administrative unit evaluates the environmental impacts of its own activities. The results serve as the basis for subsequent programs, and this multitude of data means situations are well documented. The administrative units identify the targets they must reach in striving towards the city's goals.

Harmonized actions

The program is designed to facilitate cooperation between Stockholm's residents and its business community, two groups considered essential to making the city a viable collective.

The program's objectives are consistent with those of the Swedish national environmental program, and are in harmony with regional public health and environmental goals.

Integration of actions and systematization of processes

As part of their current operations, administrative units must take into account the targets for their own activities as well as evaluate the environmental impacts of these activities. Since January 2008, all planning or follow-up has been done with the help of an on-line tool that allows each unit to integrate the objectives of the city's environmental program in planning its activities. This tool also serves to evaluate how well goals are met.

Specialist support

The mandate of Stockholm's Environment and Health Administration is to help administrative units reach the environmental program's targets in their work. As well, it helps the city's executive committee compile and analyse the data gathered via indicators.

CHAPTER 11

Critical Views on the Nordic Countries' Policies

Rates of poverty in the developed countries and the United Nations Human Poverty Index show that, overall, the Nordic countries are the best at limiting inequalities, and in particular child poverty. We have reviewed the Nordic policies that likely contributed to this success. It would be risky, however, to attribute this success to a single policy, or even a set of policies. In public health, as in economics, the complex interaction of many factors must be taken into account. Therefore it is useful to examine the limits of policies as determinants of health, and put various critiques of the viability of the Nordic model into perspective. The gaps in a variety of policies and programs and some of their unintended effects are also worthy of mention.

Conditions favouring the emergence of Nordic social policies

The coexistence of several factors have possibly given the Nordic countries the economic or socio-historic means to build welfare states, and allowed the establishment, over the course of decades, of practices predisposing people to make fair choices.

What is certain is that at a moment in their history, the Nordic countries had a combination of factors favouring the emergence of social policies. Some of these conditions resemble those that exist in Quebec, including the following six:

- The small size of the Nordic states (with populations ranging in size from 5.1 to 9.7 million inhabitants) and their tradition of solidarity, which facilitate innovative experiments in resolving the problems of poverty.
- Industrialization oriented towards leading-edge sectors, which generate better incomes for workers than do traditional industries.

- The very strong economic growth of Sweden in the 1950s, 1960s, and 1970s, which paved the way for important social reforms encouraging the distribution of wealth.
- The existence of major natural resources, particularly oil in Norway and wood in Finland, and of pork production in Denmark.
- The fact that Sweden was neutral in the last two world wars, leaving it less impoverished than the other European countries.
- A relatively small immigrant population until quite recently. Immigrants, today, represent percentages of the population varying from four percent in Finland to 14 percent in Sweden (12 percent in Quebec). The countries did not, until recently, have to deal with the problem of poverty amongst immigrants, who might have more difficulty finding work and integrating socially and economically.

The viability of the Nordic model

During the 1990s, before Sweden succeeded in correcting its economic situation, the Nordic model, and particularly the Swedish model, was subject to several critiques. The country was then in the throes of its worst recession since the 1930s. Several observers blamed this downturn, at least in part, on the high cost of social protection.

The economic situation

Since then, Sweden has righted its economic situation. In 2006, its growth rate — the annual rate of growth of GDP — was four percent, twice that of the European Union; and in 2010, it was 5.7 percent. In spite of budget cuts, privatizations, and restrictions, Sweden has also demonstrated that, just like the other Nordic countries, it can keep social protection at the heart of its policies. As a balance is struck between socio-democratic ideals and the changes wrought by global capitalism, the help and benefits offered have become less generous than they were in the 1970s and 1980s. According to the Montreal Economic Institute: "Since the mid-1990s, Sweden's economic growth has exceeded that of most other OECD countries, including Canada. According to official statistics, the employment rate is higher and inflation remains low. Public finances are in good shape, with net public debt among the world's lowest."[1]

---

1. Labrie, Y. How to explain the success of the Swedish model? Montreal Economic Institute, Economic Note, July 2007, p. 1.

Just about the same claim can be made for Nordic countries as a whole. According to the annual reports of the World Economic Forum on competitiveness, since the mid-2000s and until this day, Sweden, Norway, Finland, and Denmark have been ranking among the fifteen most competitive economies in the world with often one or more ranking among the top five. This success can be explained partly by certain characteristics of the Nordic model: transparent and efficient public institutions, solid public finances, and good macroeconomic conditions. In rankings by Gross Domestic Product per capita, the most recent (2012) Eurostat data also put the Nordic countries in enviable positions — in second, seventh, and tenth places. (See Table 11.1)

TABLE 11.1

Ranking by GDP per capita in the European Union

Country	Ranking by GDP per capita in the EU (27 countries) in purchasing power standards (PPS)
Luxemburg	1st
Norway	**2nd**
Switzerland	3rd
Austria	4th
Ireland	5th
Netherlands	6th
Sweden and Denmark	**7th**
Germany	8th
Belgium	9th
Finland and Iceland	**10th**

To date, evidently, criticisms of the Nordic model on the grounds of its prohibitive costs are unfounded. In 2003, Lefebvre was already re-assessing the claim made by some that, as the free market economy grew more dominant, this model could not survive.

In the 1990s (...) in a world where the market economy seemed to exclude a high level of social protection (...) and the dominant discourse advocated stimulating economic growth by lightening the responsibilities of businesses and lowering taxes, the Nordic societies seemed to be based on outmoded models. The Nordic welfare state, therefore, could not go hand in hand with sustained economic performances. But reality refuted this reasoning. Overall, the standard of life in the Nordic countries has remained distinctly better than the average in the EU, and economic performances remain above average.[2]

Recent economic data cast a positive light on Nordic countries' place on the world stage, and on the role of the Nordic model in explaining their success. According to Bernard and Boucher (2007), providing and managing good social protection means employing a large number of workers in public services, thus avoiding depreciation of these services and of the service sector in general. An economy in which a large proportion of the population is employed is a productive economy, and high public expenses, when incurred in the form of social investments, can result in high competitiveness.

The durability of the Nordic model is sometimes challenged by the aging of the active population, globalization of market, and heightened competition in the production and services sectors. This model is based on high taxes supporting public services that improve wage earners' quality of life and productivity. According to Nilsson and Nyström (2006), though tax hikes succeeded in getting Sweden out of the recession of the 1990s, if would be difficult to make such hikes acceptable today:

> As long as the improvement in standard of life went hand-in-hand with a lev-eling-out of income inequality, the public service managed to satisfy citizens' demands, and citizens accepted paying more taxes as their incomes rose — on the condition, however, that the growth in salaries was more or less equal for the whole society, as it was during the 30-year period following the end of the Second World War. As soon as incomes for some groups grew more rapidly than for others, the more well-to-do classes felt growing dissatisfaction with the public sector, and this lessened their tolerance of high taxes, and encouraged them to supplement the collective system with private solutions.[3]

Recent evaluations of the confidence of Nordic societies in their political institutions allow measurement, at least to some extent, of dissatisfaction with taxation rates. Though the linkage between satisfaction with tax rates and confidence in political institutions is indirect, 2010 statistics show that the Nordic countries do well when it comes to satisfaction with governance.

---

2. Lefebvre, A. Peut-on tirer des enseignements du modèle nordique ? *Revue française des affaires sociales*, vol. 4, n° 4, 2003, p. 177, free translation.
3. Nilsson, A. and Ö. Nyström. L'avenir du compromis social-démocrate – L'État-providence comme outil de transformation sociale. *La Vie des idées*, no. 15, September 2006, free translation.

The OECD's new Better Life Index evaluates, among other factors, the quality of governance as measured by the trust people have in political institutions. Sweden is ranked in second place in OECD countries by the quality of governance indicator and, moreover, 65 percent of Swedes say they trust their political institutions (the average for the OECD is 56 percent). Denmark, Finland, and Norway also scored well above the average, with 75 percent, 82 percent, and 68 percent, respectively. Following the publication of the 2010 Legatum Prosperity Index, which ranked Norway at the top of 110 countries for its people's prosperity and personal well-being, Norway was even the subject of an article entitled "Happy to Pay Taxes."[4] Swedes are also happy to pay taxes, because they trust the government and know that they get their money's worth.[5]

The viability of the Swedish model has also been challenged by some authors advancing the argument of social fragmentation. According to Kalinowski (2006), for example, Sweden, like all developed countries, is subject to the transformations of capitalism, and the Swedish job market is becoming increasingly segregated. "The economic transformations that explain the increase in productivity generate the same cleavages as in France between the competitive, the protected, the vulnerable, and the excluded. (...) The performance of the global economy hides growing disparities between regions, sectors, and social groups."[6]

On a more optimistic note, one can consider the results of the Legatum Institute. It evaluates prosperity in countries using a composite index which measures not only economic but also social factors, including social capital (social cohesion, trust). Its measurement of social capital includes an evaluation of the level of confidence citizens have in each other. The Nordic countries were at the top of a list of the 142 countries ranked in the 2014 Legatum Prosperity Index, with Norway in first place, Denmark in third, Finland in fifth, and Sweden in eleventh.

---

4. Gulfnews.com. "Happy to pay taxes," available at http://gulfnews.com/gn-focus/norway/happy-to-pay-taxes-1.806206, 2011.
5. Fouché, G. (2008). "Where tax goes up to 60 per cent, and everybody's happy paying it," *The Guardian*, Sunday November 16; and Swedish Institute (2013). "A highly trusted public body", web page available at https://sweden.se/society/why-swedes-are-okay-with-paying-taxes/.
6. Kalinowski, W. *"Pourquoi les Suédois ont-ils des raisons de s'inquiéter,"* 2006. [www.laviedesidees.fr/Pourquoi-les-Suedois-ont-ils-des.html]

The changing Swedish values of solidarity and equality

At the beginning of the 2000s, observers noticed that Sweden's passion for equality was not what it had been. Among other changes, they noted an intensification of individualistic trends, and an increase in the top salaries, leading to greater financial inequalities.

Since then, certain groups have lost confidence in the future of the welfare state, and there are questions as to whether a high level of social protection can be maintained. More than before, middle-class workers turn towards individual solutions, such as complementary retirement pension plans, to supplement the public social security system. This effectively threatens the legitimacy of systems financed by fiscal levies. As Kalinowski explains, "The situation thus seems paradoxical. While international studies highlight its macroeconomic performance, Sweden's social model is threatened from within by a crisis of confidence and solidarity, which pushes it to weaken some of this model's most characteristic traits."[7]

Moreover, the organizations that support social democracy can be seen to be moving away from their traditional working-class base, and to be increasingly open to alliance with the middle class. As well, voices have been raised against the new directions of some public policies that have been formulated in an effort to adapt to current globalization, and in reaction to the recession of the 1990s. The weakening of the social protection system could erode social cohesion and, in the long term, challenge the Swedish model of governance. According to Grjebine and Laurent (2008), "the fear of this regression might have launched excessive policies in an effort to adapt to the world and European contexts and such policies might be liable to weaken social cohesion and, finally, compromise Sweden's long-term development."[8]

Despite the several breaches visible in Swedish solidarity, the social capital remains high, as we noted above. Moreover, the Nordic countries have among the lowest incarceration rates in Europe. This can be considered an indicator of inclusion and social cohesion. As for the fears of too great an erosion of the social protection system, the fact is that total social expenditures in Sweden, expressed as a percentage of GDP in 2014,

7. Kalinowski, W. *Pourquoi les Suédois ont-ils des raisons de s'inquiéter.* 2006. [www.lavie-desidees.fr/Pourquoi-les-Suedois-ont-ils-des.html], free translation.
8. Grjebine, A. and É. Laurent. La méthode suédoise: la cohésion sociale au défi de l'adaptation. *Les Études du CERI*, no. 147, September 2008, p. 19, free translation.

remained higher than the average for the OECD countries: 28 percent compared to 21 percent. Of the 34 OECD countries, Sweden is in seventh place. Finland, Denmark, and Norway (with its particularly high GDP per capita), are in second, fourth, and seventeenth place, respectively.

As well as these data, which help assess the persistence and viability of the Nordic model, it is considered that what still distinguishes the Swedish and Nordic ways of doing things from other countries' is their overall logic. The quest for equity is still a central goal, as is the offer of enough resources to give individuals the means to overcome obstacles and develop their potential.

Gaps and unintended effects of certain policies

Though the Nordic countries' policies are inspiring in many respects, it is nonetheless the case that not all their consequences have been positive.

Gender inequality in the public and private sectors

The high rate of employment among women in Sweden is, in large measure, attributable to the jobs they hold in the public sector. Since this is the main sector in which organizational culture recognizes that time must be dedicated to the family, this is where one finds women. The Swedish job market, for this reason, is one of the most sexually segregated in the West with men working mainly in the private sector, and women in the public sector. This forces us to reconsider how domestic tasks and care-giving are shared between men and women; it could be more equal than it is.

Still vulnerable populations

After the Swedish social programs were reformed in the 1990s, an exhaustive evaluation of the social situation showed that these reforms had unintended consequences on three vulnerable populations: youth, immigrants, and single mothers. In 2007, since Sweden had not yet managed to assure real income security for youth and immigrants, it launched a program to give them access to jobs. This program also was aimed at activating a fourth group of excluded persons, the long-term unemployed.

In Denmark the proportion of those 16-to-24 years old who are at risk of poverty was 28 percent in 2010, the highest rate in Europe, where the average rate was 20 percent. In the other Nordic countries, the proportion of the population in this same age bracket who are at risk of poverty is double the proportion of the whole population at risk of poverty.

The difficulties of including immigrants

Integration of immigrants, and particularly integration into the job market, remains fragile in the Nordic countries. In Denmark, for example, half of all welfare recipients in 2003 were immigrants. In 2008, 56 percent of those living in underprivileged neighbourhoods were immigrants.

One OECD report on the economy of Sweden (2007) mentioned that job regulations in force there were designed for a homogeneous population. The level of job security in Sweden is so high that employers hesitate to hire people with whose profiles they are not familiar, for they could incur significant costs if such persons were not to meet expectations.

A hardening of attitudes towards marginalized populations, and in particular towards immigrants, especially when they benefit from welfare, can be observed in some Nordic milieus.

Two examples of programs with lukewarm results

Evaluations of two Swedish social programs — one for insertion of the homeless, the other for helping residents of underprivileged neighbour- hoods — showed lukewarm results.

The programs for inserting the homeless, following the so-called 'staircase of transition' approach, entailed encouraging homeless persons to enter a process of transition, at the end of which they would be living in their own apartments in complete autonomy. A homeless person would first be offered lodging in a closely supervised community hostel, then in a residence with social reinsertion services, and so on until all the steps of the staircase had been climbed, and the goal, a perfectly autonomous life, reached. But, according to several evaluations, this system runs up against the obstacle that the categorization of housing arrangements is incompat- ible with homeless realities. Few people qualify as semi-autonomous and can access residences reserved for those so qualified. Many people are not autonomous and yet, because resources are insufficient, remain without support.

A program of aid for the residents of underprivileged neighbour- hoods was implemented in the greater Stockholm region. The government invested in reducing the disadvantages of certain neighbourhoods by helping residents find work or get training. These services could be adapted to immigrants' needs. An evaluation of this program showed that, after their lot had improved, residents moved to better neighbourhoods, only to be replaced in their old neighbourhood by less advantaged persons. The program had positive effects for those who left their old neighbourhood. However, in terms of the goal of increasing social diversity, the results were negative. Contrary to the aims of the urban policies, the targeted neighbourhoods have remained ghettos.

CONCLUSION

Inequalities in Health: Report of a Research Working Group, better known as the *Black Report* after its principal author, Sir Douglas Black — was published in England in 1980. This report definitively established the reality of social inequalities in health: it showed that mortality rates for men at the bottom of the social hierarchy were double those for men at the top. The Whitehead, Acheson, and Marmot reports, published in 1987, 1998, and 2010 respectively, set forth the same conclusions. Since then, many studies have shown that this reality applies to multiple health problems in diverse societies. In short, with very few exceptions, the incidence of cancers, cardiovascular diseases, infectious diseases, and trauma is higher among the poor.

Must we see this as fate? Certainly not; the most recent studies on the subject define several strategies for reducing health inequalities. They show that narrowing the health gaps between rich and poor leads to a healthier population. The strategies for improving health equality go hand in hand with social inclusion and strengthened bonds of trust between people, with higher rates of academic success, low rates of incarcerations, and considerable upward social mobility.

In all categories of such advances, the champions are the Nordic societies; they combine low rates of social inequalities and excellent health results with great economic competitiveness and unparalleled environmental performance. The governance model and social policies these countries have developed are what we have attempted to explain in this work.

The characteristics of this model are as follows:

1. Emphasis on prevention and extensive social protection.
2. Integration of social policies in multiple fields of action.

3. Policies that encourage a high rate of employment and a relatively equal distribution of incomes.
4. Integration of gender equity in all public policies.
5. Policies that recognize the multiple facets of a life course.
6. Political decisions informed by evidence-based data and a tradition of social and health research.
7. Political processes carried out with a significant degree of local democracy and with respect for strong workers' unions.
8. Political processes based on multiparty democratic representation and a proportional representation electoral system that encourage citizen power.
9. Tradition of consensus decision making.

These distinctive traits of the Nordic model are expressed in such policies as family, housing, gender equity, education, social inclusion, and sustainable development policies.

Family policies and policies for balancing responsibilities at home and at work contain generous measures that allow great flexibility and equalize opportunities both for children, and for mothers and fathers. These policies acknowledge that, in a spirit of collective parenting solidarity, parents alone are not responsible for taking care of and educating children and government intervention is also required.

The policies of housing aid constitute a central element in social protection. They assume that all citizens have the right to live in decent lodging and in a high-quality environment. These policies fit into the sustainable development perspective; in some countries, they are the responsibility of the environment ministry. These policies have the explicit goal of counterbalancing the free market so that the housing market is stable and balanced, and can serve all social strata and all geographic sectors. The result of these policies is that public housing accounts for 20 percent of the entire residential market.

The gender equity policies are designed to take an integrated approach and are endorsed by wide consensus. These policies aim at equalizing opportunity by encouraging the desexualization of roles, financial autonomy, and individual and collective power and influence. Their application is supervised by several consultative and monitoring organizations.

Education policies entail significant investments: between 6.2 and 7.5 percent of GDP. They ensure equal opportunities for all students. Great

importance is attributed to education — as demonstrated by the low drop-
out rate in Finland, one percent — and the universality of access. Priority
is given to the quality of the public education system, and there are few
private schools. Policies stress early interventions and facilitate access to
special education for a large number of students — almost one student in
five in Finland. The policies reflect a concept of education whereby stu-
dents should learn about life, develop self-esteem, learn throughout their
entire lives, update their know-how, acquire new skills and, in so doing,
eventually contribute to the economy.

The policies of social inclusion encourage not only the integration of
individuals with difficulties, such as handicapped persons, drug addicts,
those with very low incomes, the unemployed, and the homeless, but also
individuals temporarily less available for work, such as parents of young
children, caregivers, and students. Their goal is to reduce the vulnerability
not only of the excluded but also of citizens at various phases of their lives.
Using measures such as paid parental leave, financial aid for students, old-
age pensions, and employment insurance, these policies aim to equalize
individuals' means. Thus governments often make no distinction between
inclusion strategies and social protection measures. These policies apply
in multiple sectors, and count heavily on integration in employment,
empowerment, autonomy, and financial independence. These policies also
stress the idea of the duty of having a job as one of the main ways in which
citizens contribute to society.

The policies of sustainable development are based on a comprehensive
vision in which the common good, health, and the economy play major
roles. Cities intervene heavily through their programs and investments,
and by negotiating support and the necessary funds with other levels of
government. Initiatives at the local level are supported by laws and by the
national government. Responsibility in many fields is assigned to the level
of municipalities which, in consequence, are major players in sustainable
development. Plans and goals are based on summaries of knowledge and
evaluations made both before and after interventions. These goals are
attained by mobilizing not only municipal employees, but also the business
community, the research and technology sector and, of course, citizens.
The process is carried out in a spirit of democracy and consultation, and
encourages the circulation of scientific information.

The social policies of the Nordic countries are worth exploring. Though
it is true that they cannot be transposed as is, they serve, nonetheless, as

inspiring examples for Quebec and for other Western societies. Knowing about alternative and successful ways of doing things, and about the principles on which they are designed and implemented, is unquestionably an asset in the quest for a just and healthy society.

Bibliography

Acheson, D. *Independent Inquiry Into Inequalities in Health*. London, The Stationery Office, 1998.

Adler, N.E. and J. Stewart. Preface to the biology of disadvantage: socioeconomic status and health. *Annals of the New York Academy of Sciences,* vol. 1186, February 2010, p. 1-4.

Ahlborn, M. All aspects on the residential rent negotiating process. Akelius University, April 2011. [university.akelius.de/library/pdf/all_aspect_ahlborn_mi1104.pdf]

Allen Consulting Goup, The. *Are we there yet: indicators of inequality in health*. Report to Department of Human Services, Australia, 2008.

American Public Health Association. Built Environment and Health. *American Journal of Public Health*, vol. 93, no. 9, September 2003.

Anderson, S.A. Core indicators of nutritional status for difficult-to-sample populations. *Journal of Nutrition*, vol. 120, no. 11, 1990, p. 1559-1600.

Andersson, R. and Å. Bråmå. Selective migration in Swedish distressed neighbourhoods: can area-based urban policies counteract segregation processes? *Housing Studies,* vol. 19, no. 4, 2004, p. 517-539.

Anxo, D., L. Flood and Y. Kocoglu. Offre de travail and répartition des activités domestiques and parentales au sein du couple: une comparaison entre la France and la Suède. *Économie and statistique*, no. 352-353, 2002, p. 127-150.

Araya, R. et al. Common mental disorders and the built environment in Santiago, Chile. *The British Journal of Psychiatry*, vol. 190, 2007, p. 394-401.

Barbier, J.-C. Les politiques d'activation des pays scandinaves and l'expérience française. *Revue française des affaires sociales*, vol. 4, no. 4, 2003, p. 187-192.

Bartley, M. *Health Inequality: An Introduction to Theories, Concepts and Methods*. Polity Press, Cambridge (UK), 2004.

Beck, C.W. *Education Otherwise and Home Education in Norway*. University of Oslo, 2000. [folk.uio.no/cbeck/EDUCATION%20OTHERWISE%20IN%20NORWAY.htm]

Bergström, G.L. et al. Sickness presenteeism today, sickness, absenteeism tomorrow? A prospective study on sickness presenteeism and future sickness absenteeism. *Journal of Occupational and Environmental Medicine*, vol. 51, no. 6, 2009, p. 629-638.

Bernard, P. and G. Boucher. Institutional competitiveness, social investment, and welfare regimes. *Regulation and Governance*, vol. 1, no. 3, September 2007, p. 213-229.

Bernard, P. and S. McDaniel. *The Lifecourse as a Policy Lens: Challenges and Opportunities.* Ottawa, Human Resources and Social Development Canada, 2008.

Bernard, P. and S. Saint-Arnaud. Du pareil au même ? La position des quatre principales provinces canadiennes dans l'univers des régimes providentiels. *Canadian Journal of Sociology/Cahiers canadiens de sociologie*, vol. 29, no. 2, 2004.

Bernard, P. et al. Capturing the lifecourse: The contribution of a panel study of lifecourse dynamics (PSLD) to public policy analysis in Canada. *Proceedings of the Conference on Longitudinal Social and Health Surveys in an International Perspective*, Montreal, January 2006, 98 p.

Björklund, A. et al. Brother correlations in earnings in Denmark, Finland, Norway, and Sweden compared to United States. *Journal of Population Economics*, vol. 15, 2002, p. 757-772.

Brachet, S. *Politique familiale and assurance parentale en Suède: une synthèse.* Institut national d'études démoraphiques, Paris, 2001.

Brachet, S. *Le congé parental en Suède: implications pour la garde d'enfants de moins de trois ans.* Paris, Institut national d'études démographiques, 2002.

Brännström, L. Poor places, poor prospects? Counterfactual models of neighbourhood effects on social exclusion in Stockholm, Sweden. *Urban Studies*, vol. 41, no. 13, 2004, p. 2515-2537.

Brunekreef, B. and S.T. Holgate. Air pollution and health. *Lancet*, vol. 360, 2002, p. 1233-1242.

Buhigas Schubert, C. and H. Martens. *The Nordic model: A recipe for European success?* European Policy Centre, Brussels, 2005. [http://www.isn.ethz.ch/Digital-Library/Publications/Detail/?ots591=0c54e3b3-1e9c-be1e-2c24-a6a8c7060233&lng=en&id=13888]

Canada. Canada Mortgage and Housing Corporation. Family Homelessness: Causes and Solutions. *Research Highlight*, July 2003. [http://www.cmhc-schl.gc.ca/odpub/pdf/63221.pdf?fr=1283201777625]

Canada. Employment and Social Development Canada. *Indicators of Well-being in Canada. Work - Unionization Rates.* 2012. [http://www4.hrsdc.gc.ca/.3nd.3c.1t.4r@-eng.jsp?iid=17]

Canada. Public Health Agency of Canada. *Sustainable Development Strategy 2007-2010*, November. 2006. [www.phac-aspc.gc.ca/publicat/sds-sdd/sds-sdd2-a-eng.php]

Canada. Parlement du Canada. *Renseignements intéressants sur les élections fédérales – Femmes*, 2011. [www.parl.gc.ca/Parlinfo/Compilations/ElectionsAndRidings/TriviaWomen.aspx?Language=F]

Canada. Parliament of Canada. Federal Election Trivia: women [http://www.parl.gc.ca/Parlinfo/Compilations/ElectionsAndRidings/TriviaWomen.aspx?Language=E]

Chartrand, S. *Les leçons du système préscolaire suédois*. Rapport de recherche, Centre de recherche Léa-Roback sur les inégalités sociales de santé, Montréal, 2011.

Chen, J. *The Dynamics of Housing Allowance Claims in Sweden: A discrete-time hazard analysis*. Working Paper 1, Uppsala University, Department of Economics, 2006.

Chittleborough, C.R. et al. Monitoring inequities in self-rated health over the life course in population surveillance systems. *American Journal of Public Health*, vol. 99, no. 4, 2009, p. 680-689.

Christiansen, T. Reducing inequality in health through prevention. *Health Policy Monitor*, no. 12, 2008, p. 1-7.

CIRIUS Denmark. *The Danish Education System*, ministère de l'Éducation du Danemark, 2006.

Cities Climate Leadership Group. Stockholm's clean vehicles are slashing 200,000 tons Co2 annually. 2010.

Claussen, B., G. Davey Smith and D. Thellen. Impact of childhood and adulthood socioeconomic position on cause specific mortality: the Oslo Mortality Study. *Journal of Epidemiology and Community Health*, vol. 1, no. 57, 2003, p. 40-45.

Cleantech Group. *Top 10 Cleantech Cluster Organizations for 2010*. 2010.

Collin, C. and H. Jensen. *Profil statistique de la pauvreté au Canada*. Library of Parliament. Social Affairs Division, 2009. [www.parl.gc.ca/Content/LOP/ResearchPublications/prb0917-f.htm#a2]

Conference Board of Canada. *How Canada Performs 2009: A Report Card on Canada*. 2010. [http://www.conferenceboard.ca/e-library/abstract.aspx?did=3526]

Conference Board of Canada. Society–Child Poverty, 2011. [www.conferenceboard.ca/hcp/Details/society/child-poverty.aspx]

Cookson, C. Poverty mars formation of infant brains. *The Financial Times*, February 16, 2008. [www.ft.com/intl/cms/s/0/62c45126-dc1f-11dc-bc82-0000779fd2ac.html#axzz2YfGvRPoQ]

Copenhagen. *Cycle Policy 2002–2012*. 2002.

Copenhagen. *Copenhagen's Green Accounts 2007*. 2007.

Copenhagen. *Eco-Metropolis–Our Vision for Copenhagen 2015*, Technical and Environmental Administration, 2007. [http://kk.sites.itera.dk/apps/kk_pub2/pdf/674_CFbnhMePZr.pdf] (Unpaginated)

Copenhagen. *Application for European Green Capital, 2008*.

Copenhagen. *Plan C–Fact sheet, 2009*.

Copenhagen. *Copenhagen Cleantech Cluster–Fact sheet, 2009*.

Copenhagen. *Business Related Activities in Copenhagen–Fact sheet, 2009*.

Côté, S.M. et al. The role of maternal education and nonmaternal care services in the prevention of children's physical aggression problems. *Archives of General Psychiatry*, vol. 64, no. 11, November 2007, p. 1305-1312.

Cousineau, M.-È. Au sein de l'entreprise. *Jobboom.com, le magazine*, vol 6, no. 2, 2005. [www.jobboom.com/jobmag/2005/v6n2/v6n2-03.html]

Crooks, D. American children at risk: Poverty and its consequences for children's health, growth, and school achievement. *Yearbook of Physical Anthropology*, vol. 38, no. S2, 1995, p. 57-86.

Cummins, S.K. and R.J. Jackson. The built environment and children's health. *Pediatric Clinics of North America*, vol. 48, no. 5, 2001, p. 1241-1252.

Dah, E. Disability and employment: sustainability of 'the Nordic model'. *European Journal of Public Health*, vol. 20, no. 4, 2010, p. 370-371.

Deletang, N. Les régimes de protection sociale de trois pays nordiques: Danemark, Finlande, Suède. *Revue française des affaires sociales*, vol. 4, 2003, p. 529-543.

Denmark. Statistics Denmark. *Declarations of content: Housing benefits (rent benefits).* 2011. [dst.dk]

Denmark. Ministry of Social Affairs, Ministry of Interior Affairs and Health. *National Report on Strategies for Social Protection and Social Inclusion.* 2006. [www.sm.dk/data/Lists/Publikationer/Attachments/321/National_report_on_strategies.pdf]

Denmark. *Government and politics.* 2007. [www.denmark.dk/en/menu/AboutDenmark/GovernmentPolitics/]

Denmark. Ministry of Social Affairs, Ministry of Interior Affairs and Health. *Distribution of tasks at state, county and local levels, 2007.* [www.im.dk]

Denmark. Ministry of Social Affairs, Ministry of Interior Affairs and Health. *National Report on Strategies for Social Protection and Social Inclusion.* 2006. [www.sm.dk/data/Lists/Publikationer/Attachments/321/National_report_on_strategies.pdf]

Denmark. Ministry of Social Affairs, Ministry of Interior Affairs and Health. *National Report on Strategies for Social Protection and Social Inclusion 2008-2010.* September 2008.

Desrosiers, H. et al. *Enquête de nutrition auprès des enfants québécois de 4 ans.* Institut de la statistique du Québec, 2005.

Devos, L. and M. Meskel-Cresta. *À la découverte du système éducatif finlandais.* ambassade finlandaise en France, 2004. [www.info-finlande.fr/societe/education/article/A_la_decouverte_du_systeme_educatif.html]

Dow,W.H. and D.H. Rehkopf. Socioeconomic gradients in health in international and historical context. *Annals of the New York Academy of Sciences*, vol. 1186, February 2010, p. 24-36.

Dubois, L. et al. Family food insufficiency is related to overweight among preschoolers. *Social Science & Medicine*, vol. 63, no. 6, September 2006, p. 1503-1516.

Dyb, E. and K. Johannessen. *Homeless in Norway – A survey.* Norwegian Institute for Urban and Regional Research, 2009.

Edgar, B. *Norway 2006–National Strategy to Prevent and Tackle Homelessness. The Pathway to a Permanent Home–Synthesis Report.* European Commission – DG Employment, Social Affairs and Equal Opportunities, 2006.

Ejsing, P., P. Joergensen and R. Oehlenschlaeger. *Denmark – State of the art; Architecture and Sustainability in Danish Housing.* European Commission, 2003.

Ekonomifakta. GDP – Gross Domestic Product, 2011. [www.ekonomifakta.se/en/Facts-and-figures/Economy/Economic-growth/GDP/]

Emerson, J. et al. *2010 Environmental Performance Index*. Yale University, 2010. [epi.yale.edu]

Esty, D. et al. *2008 Environmental Performance Index*. Yale University, 2008. [epi.yale.edu]

Esty, D. et al. *2005 Environmental Sustainability Index: Benchmarking National Environmental Stewardship*. Yale Center for Environmental Law and Policy, New Haven, 2005.

EURinfo. Le travail entre flexibilité and sécurité. *Le magazine de la Représentation de la Commission européenne en Belgique,* no. 310, November 2006.

Eurocities Working Group on Homelessness and Housing. *Cities' Strategies Against Homelessness–First report of the Eurocities Working Group on Homelessness*. Eurocities, 2006.

Eurocities Working Group on Homelessness and Housing. *Cities' Strategies Against Homelessness–First report of the Eurocities Working Group on Homelessness*, Eurocities, 2008. [http://www.eukn.org/dsresource?objectid=148178].

European Commission. *Avance sur le terme de la pension alimentaire*. Emploi and Affaires sociales – MISSOC, 2002.

European Commission. *The Expert Panel's Evaluation Work and Final Recommendations for the European Green Capital Award of 2010 and 2011*. European Commission, Directorate-General for the Environment, January 23, 2009.

European Commission. *La protection sociale dans les États membres de l'UE and de l'Espace économique européen – Situation au 1er janvier 2002 and évolution*. 2002.

European Industrial Relations Observatory on-line (EIRO). *Government launches job package to tackle social exclusion*. Eurofound, 2007. [www.eurofound.europa.eu/eiro/2007/05/articles/se0705019i.htm]

European Urban Knowledge Network. *Cities' Strategies Against Homelessness–First report of a Eurocities Working Group*. Eurocities, 2008.

Eurostast. Minimum wage statistics. European Commission, 2011. [epp.eurostat.ec.europa.eu/statistics_explained/index.php/Minimum_wage_statistics]

Eurostat. *Combating Poverty and Social Exclusion: A Statistical Portrait of the European Union 2010*. European Commission, 2010.

Eurothine. *Tackling Health Inequalities in Europe: an Integrated Approach–Eurothine–Final Report*. Department of Public Health–University Medical Centre Rotterdam, Netherlands, 2007.

Evans, G.W. and P. Kim. Multiple risk exposure as a potential explanatory mechanism for the socioeconomic status-health gradient. *Annals of the New York Academy of Sciences*, vol. 1186, February 2010, p. 174-189.

Ewing, R. et al. Relationship between urban sprawl and physical activity, obesity, and morbidity. *American Journal of Health Promotion*, vol. 18, no. 1, September-October. 2003, p. 47-57.

Family and Parenting Support Thematic Working Group, The. *Family Policies that work best for Children–Fighting Child Poverty and Promoting Child Well-being.* Eurochild, 2010.

Finland. Ministry of the Environment. *Housing, 2007.* [www.environment.fi/default.asp?node=4073&lan=en]. [FAULTY LINK]

Finland. Finnish National Board of Education. *Development of the Finnish education system between 1960 and 2004.* 2004. [www.oph.fi/english/]

Finland. Finnish National Board of Education. *Education and the Finnish society.* 2011. [www.oph.fi/english/sources_of_information/international_assessments/pisa/education_and_the_finnish_society]

Finland. Finnish National Board of Education. *PISA–Programme for International Students Assessment, 2011.* [www.oph.fi/english/sources_of_information/pisa]

Finland. *Housing allowances, 2007.* [www.suomi.fi/suomifi/english]

Finland. *Central government agencies and public bodies.* 2011. [www.suomi.fi/suomifi/english/state_and_municipalities/state_administration_and_central_government/central_government_agencies_and_public_bodies/index.html]

Finland. Housing Finance and Development Centre of Finland. *The Housing Finance and Development Centre of Finland* (ARA), 2011. [www.ara.fi]

Finland. Ministry of the Environment. *Housing,* 2007. [www.environment.fi/default.asp?node=4073&lan=en].

France. Ministère français de l'Écologie, de l'Énergie, du Développement durable and de l'Aménagement. *Björkhagen: Villa urbaine durable, voyage d'étude en Scandinavie, 1994–1996.* [www.chantier.net/vud/vudbjk.htm]

Franco, A, C. Álvarez-Dardet and M.T. Ruiz. Effect of democracy on health: ecological study. *British Medical Journal*, vol. 329, no. 7480, December 2004, p. 1421-1423.

Frank, L., M.A. Andresen and T.L. Schmid. Obesity relationships with community design, physical activity and time spent in cars. *American Journal of Prevention Medicine,* vol. 27, no. 2, August 2004, p. 87-96.

Frohlich, K. et al. *Les inégalités sociales de santé au Québec.* Presses de l'Université de Montréal, 2008.

Galano, F. *Approches comparatives des congés de naissance entre la France et ses voisins scandinaves.* 2006. [www.tripalium.com/gazette/Gazette2006/Escem2006/gala01.asp]

Galtry, J. and P. Callister Assessing the optimal length of parental leave for child and parental well-being; How can research inform policy? *Journal of Family Issues,* vol. 26, no. 2, 2005, p. 219-246.

Galtry, J. The impact on breastfeeding of labour market policy and practice in Ireland, Sweden, and the USA. *Social Science & Medicine,* vol. 57, no. 1, July 2003, p. 167-177.

Gaulejac, Vincent de. *Les sources de la honte.* Desclée de Brouwer, Paris, 1996, 315 p.

Geoffroy, M. et al. Non-maternal care reduces cognitive inequalities for children disadvantaged family backgrounds: evidences population-based study. *International Society for the Study of Behavioural Development* (ISSBD), Wüzberg (Allemagne), 2008.

Grjebine, A. and É. LaurentLa méthode suédoise: la cohésion sociale au défi de l'adaptation. *Les Études du CERI*, no. 147, September 2008.

Gulf News. Happy to pay taxes. 2011. [gulfnews.com/gn-focus/norway/happy-to-pay-taxes-1.806206]

Gurria, A. *Divided We Stand: Why Inequality Keeps Rising.* Speech by OECD Secretary-General, December 2011. [www.oecd.org/document/22/0,3746,en_21571361_44315115_49185046_1_1_1_1,00.html]

Haines, A. et al. Public health benefits of strategies to reduce greenhouse-gas emissions: overview and implications for policy makers. *Lancet*, vol. 374, no. 9707, December 19, 2009, p. 2104-2114.

Hall, P. and S. Montin. *Governance Networks and Democracy at Regional and Local Level in Sweden (report).* Roskilde University, Center for Democratic Governance, 2007.

Hall, P. and S. Montin. *Governance Networks and Democracy at Regional and Local Level in Sweden.* Roskilde: Roskilde University, Centre for democratic network governance. Working Paper 2007:9. [www.ruc.dk/fileadmin/assets/isg/02_Forskning/demnetgov/Working_Paper_2007_9.pdf]

Helsinki. *The Helsinki Action Plan for Sustainability*, 2002.

Helsinki. The Voice of the Young in Helsinki, 2009. [http://www.hel.fi/hki/Helsinki/en/Etusivu]

Héon, L. and N. Mayrand. L'accès des femmes à un poste de direction dans des écoles secondaires de Montréal. *Recherches féministes*, vol. 16, no. 1, 2003.

Hertzman, C. The biological embedding of early experience and its effects on health in adulthood. *Annals of the New York Academy of Sciences*, vol. 896, 1999, p. 85-95.

Independent Living Institute. *Act concerning Support and Service for Persons with Certain Functional Impairments, passed on 27 May 1993–Bill 1993:387.* 1993. [www.independentliving.org/docs3/englss.html]

Intergovernmental Panel on Climate Change (IPCC). *Climate Change 2007: Impacts, Adaptation and Vulnerability – Summary for Policymakers.* Geneva, 2007.

Inter-Parliamentary Union (IPU). *Women in national parliaments: World Classification.* May 2011. [www.ipu.org/wmn-e/arc/classif310511.htm].

International Institute for Democracy and Electoral Assistance (IDEA). *Voter Turnout, 2010.* [www.idea.int/vt]

Jahnukainen, M. Two models for preventing students with special needs dropping out of education in Finland. *European Journal of Special Needs Education*, vol. 16, no. 3, 2001, p. 245-258.

Jegermalm, M. Support for carers of older people: The roles of the public and voluntary sectors in Sweden. *Social Policy and Administration*, vol. 37, no. 7, 2003, p. 756-771.

Johan, A. and R. Van Hoofstat. *Pénurie d'habitat: Vers une rénovation de la politique du logement.* Roularta Books, Zellik (Belgique), 2011.

Johnsen, J.R. *Health Systems in Transition: Norway.* European Observatory on Health Systems and Policies, vol. 8, no. 1, 2006.

Johnson, R. Metrics and measures in tackling the social determinants of health–the example of mental health and housing. *Journal of Public Mental Health*, vol. 9, no. 3, 2010, p. 36-44.

Jones, S.J. et al. Traffic calming policy can reduce inequalities in child pedestrian injuries: database study. *Injury Prevention*, vol. 11, no. 3, juin 2005, p. 152-156.

Jørgensen, H. Le rôle des syndicats dans les réformes sociales en Scandinavie dans les années quatre-vingt-dix. *Revue française des affaires sociales*, vol. 4, no. 4, 2003, p. 121-150.

Kalinowski, W. *Pourquoi les Suédois ont-ils des raisons de s'inquiéter, 2006.* [www.lavie-desidees.fr/Pourquoi-les-Suedois-ont-ils-des.html]

Kangas, O. and J. Palme. Making social policy work for economic development: the Nordic experience. *International Journal of Social Welfare*, vol. 18, April 2009, p. S62-S72.

Kawachi, I., S.V. Subramanian and N. Almeida-Filho. A glossary for health inequalities, *Journal of Epidemiology and Community Health*, vol. 56, no. 9, September 2002, p. 647-652.

Kela–The Social Insurance Institution of Finland.*Our services–Students, 2010.* [www. kela.fi/in/internet/english.nsf/NET/081001131300IL?]

Kela–The Social Insurance Institution of Finland. *Our services–Housing benefits, 2011.* [www.kela.fi/in/internet/english.nsf/NET/081101150604EH]

Knudsen, E.L. et al. Economic, neurobiological, and behavioral perspectives on building America's future workforce. *Proceedings of the National Academy of Sciences of the USA*, vol. 103, no. 27, July 5, 2006, p. 10156-10162.

Korpi, B.M. The Politics of Pre-School - intentions and decisions underlying the emergence and growth of the Swedish Pre-school. Stockholm, Ministry of Education and Research, 2007. [www.sweden.gov.se/sb/d/8746/a/91061]

Kotowska, I.E. et al. *Second European Quality of Life Survey: Family Life and Work.* European Foundation for the Improvement of Living and Working Conditons, Dublin, 2010, 96 p.

Kuh, D.L. and Y. Ben-Shlomo. *A Life Course Approach to Chronic Diseases Epidemiology– Tracing the Origins of Ill-health from Early to Adult Life.* Oxford University Press, 1997.

Laborit, H. *Éloge de la fuite.* Laffont, Paris, 1976, 233 p.

Labrie, Y. Comment expliquer le succès du modèle suédois? Institut économique de Montréal, July 2007. [www.iedm.org/files/juillet07_fr.pdf]

Lafferty, W.M. and F. Coenen. The Diffusion of Local Agenda 21 in Twelve European Countries. Paper presented at the international workshop Diffusion of Environmental Policy Innovations, Berlin, 2000.

Latkin, C.A. and Curry, A.D. Stressful neighborhoods and depression: a prospective study of the impact of neighborhood disorder. *Journal of Health and Social Behavior*, vol. 44, no. 1, March 2003, p. 34-44.

Lefebvre, A. Peut-on tirer des enseignements du modèle nordique ? *Revue française des affaires sociales*, vol. 4, no. 4, 2003, p. 177-186.

Legatum Institute. *The 2010 Legatum Prosperity Index, 2011*. [www.prosperity.com/]

Lewis, J. The decline of the male breadwinner model: implications for work and care. *Social Politics*, vol. 8, no. 2, 2001, p. 163-164.

Logan, S. and N. Spencer. Inequality and children's health. *Child: Care, Health and Development*, vol. 26, no. 1, January 2000, p. 1-3.

Lorant, V. et al. Socioeconomic inequalities in depression: a meta-analysis. *American Journal of Epidemiology*, vol. 157, no. 2, January 2003, p. 98-112.

Lundberg, O. et al. The role of welfare state principles and generosity in social policy programmes for public health: an international comparative study, *Lancet*, vol. 372, no. 9650, 2008, p. 1633-1640.

Luo, Y. and L.J. Waite. The impact of childhood and adult SES on physical, mental, and cognitive well-being in later life. *Journal of Gerontology, Series B*, vol. 60, no. 2, 2005, p. S93-S101.

Lupien, S.J. et al. Can poverty get under your skin? Basal cortisol levels and cognitive function in children from low and high socioeconomic status. *Development and Psychopathology*, vol. 13, no. 3, 2001, p. 653-676.

Lupien, S.J. et al. Child's stress hormone levels correlate with mother's socioeconomic status and depressive state. *Biological Psychiatry*, vol. 48, no. 10, 2000, p. 976-980.

Mackenbach, J.P. Socioeconomic inequalities in health in the Netherlands: impact of a five year research programme. *British Medical Journal*, vol. 309, no. 6967, 1994, p. 1487-1491.

Mackenbach, J.P and K. Stronks. The development of a strategy for tackling health inequalities in The Netherlands. *International Journal for Equity in Health*, vol. 3, no. 1, 2004.

Mandel, H. and M. Shalev. How welfare states shape the gender pay gap: a theoretical and comparative analysis, *Social Forces*, vol. 87, no. 4, 2009, p. 1873-1911.

Manning, J.E., C.J. Shogan and S.N. Smelcer. *Women in the United States Congress: 1917-2011*. Congressional Research Service, 2011.

Marmot, M. Understanding social inequalities in health. *Perspectives in Biology and Medicine*, vol. 46, no. 3, 2003, p S9-S23.

Marmot, M. *Fair Society, Healthy Lives–Strategic Review of Heatlh Inequalities in England post-2010*. UCL Institute of Health Equity, London, 2010.

Ménard, S. Finlande contre Québec – Une école de rêve. *Journal de Montréal*, March 4, 2006. [www2.canoe.com/infos/dossiers/archives/2006/03/20060304-084200.html]

Miech, R.A. et al. Trends in the association of poverty with overweight among US adolescents, 1971-2004. *Journal of the American Medical Association*, vol. 295, no. 20, 2006, p. 2385-2393.

Milner, H. *Civic Literacy: How Informed Citizens Make Democracy Work*. University Press of New England, Hanover, 2002.

Milner, H. Electoral systems, integrated institutions, and turnout in local and national elections: Canada in comparative perspective. *Canadian Journal of Political Science*, vol. 30, no. 1, 1997, p. 89-106.

Montreal. Agence de la santé and des services sociaux de Montréal. *Enquête sur la maturité scolaire des enfants montréalais – Rapport régional 2008.* Montreal, 2008, 135 p.

Montreal. Direction de la santé publique de l'Agence de santé and des services sociaux de Montréal. *Le portrait de la population montréalaise 2010.* Montreal, 2010.

Montreal. Direction de santé publique de l'Agence de la santé and des services sociaux de Montréal. *Rapport annuel 2004-2005 sur la santé de la population. Objectif jeunes: comprendre soutenir.* Montreal, 2005, 109 p.

Montreal. Direction de santé publique de l'Agence de la santé and des services sociaux de Montréal. *Rapport du directeur de santé publique 2011 – Les inégalités sociales de santé à Montréal. Le chemin parcouru.* Montreal, 2011.

Montreal. Direction de santé publique de l'Agence de la santé and des services sociaux de Montréal. *Le transport urbain, une question de santé – Rapport annuel 2006 sur la santé de la population montréalaise.* Montreal, 2006.

Morel, N. Politique sociale and égalité entre les sexes en Suède. *Recherches et prévisions*, no. 64, 2001.

Myers, F., A. McCollam and A. Woodhouse. *Addressing Mental Health Inequalities in Scotland: Equal Minds.* National Programme for Improving Mental Health and Well-Being, Scottish Development Centre for Mental Health, Edinburgh, 2005.

Nagin, D.S. and R.E. Tremblay. Parental and early childhood predictors of persistent physical aggression in boys from kindergarten to high school. *Archives of General Psychiatry*, vol. 58, 2001, p. 389-394.

Nilsson, A. and Ö. Nyström. L'avenir du compromis social-démocrate – L'État-providence comme outil de transformation sociale. *La Vie des idées*, no. 15, September 2006. [www.laviedesidees.fr/L-avenir-du-compromis-social.html]

Nordfeldt, M. and O.S. Larsson. *Local welfare in Sweden: housing, employment and child care.* Reseach report for WILCO [Welfare Innovations at the Local level in favour of Cohesion], 2011.

Nordic Council of Ministers. *Social insurance in the nordic countries.* 2009. [nordsoc.is/en/Social-insurance-in-the-Nordic-Area]

Nordic Council of Ministers. *Sustainable Development–New Bearings for the Nordic Countries.* Copenhagen, Revised edition, 2009. [http://www.regjeringen.no/upload/FIN/berekraftig/Sustainable_development.pdf]

Nordvik, V. and P. Åhrén. The Norwegian Housing Allowances–Efficiency and Effects. Paper presented at the European Network for Housing Research conference, Cambridge, United Kingdom, 2004.

Norway. Norwegian Board of Health Supervision. *Norwegian health and social services.* 2006. [www.helsetilsynet.no/templates/ArticleWithLinks_____5520.aspx]

Norway. Norwegian Labour Inspection Authority. *Guide to the Working Environment Act and the Holidays Act.* 2007.

Norway. *Husbanken. Find out if you are entitled to housing allowance.* 2011. [www.husbanken.no/english/what-is-housing-allowance/find-out-if-you-are-entitled]

Norway. Housing and property. 2007. [www.regjeringen.no/en/topics/Housing-and-property.html?id=211]

Norway. Statistiska centralbyrån. *Barnomsorg: Utbildningsstatistisk årsbok,* 2007.

Norway. *Stay in Norway. Parental benefit on earth,* 2011. [www.nav.no/English]

Norway. Ministry of Education and Research. *Equal Education in Practice!–Strategy for better teaching and greater participation of linguistic minorities in kindergartens, schools and education 2007-2009,* February 2007.

Norway. Ministry of Health and Care Services. *National strategy to reduce social inequalities in health, 2006-2007.* [www.regjeringen.no/en/dep/hod/documents/regpubl/stmeld/2006-2007/Report-No-20-2006-2007-to-the-Storting/2/2/1. html?id=466524]

[http://www.regjeringen.no/en/dep/hod/documents/regpubl/stmeld/2006-2007/Report-No-20-2006-2007-to-the-Storting.html?id=466505]

Norway. Ministry of Labour and Social Inclusion. *Action Plan for Integration and Social Inclusion of the Immigrant Population and Goals for Social Inclusion,* 2007.

O'Leary, A. Stress, emotion, and human immune function. *Psychological Bulletin,* vol. 108, no. 3, 1990, p. 363-382.

Observatoire des inégalités. *Les inégalités ne sont pas une fatalité, 2006.* [www.inegalites. fr/spip.php?article590]

OECD. *Early Childhood Education and Care Policy in Sweden.* 1999.

OECD. *Economic Surveys–Sweden.* 2007

OECD. *PISA 2006: Science Competencies for Tomorrow's World–Executive Summary.* 2007.

OECD. *Economic Surveys–Sweden.* 2007

OECD. *Croissance and inégalités. Distribution des revenus and pauvreté dans les pays de l'OCDE.* 2008

OECD. Foreign-born and foreign populations, *OECD Factbook 2010: Economic, Environmental and Social Statistics.* 2010. ISBN 92-64-08356-1.

OECD. *OECD Science, Technology and Industry Outlook 2010.* [www.oecd.org/dataoecd/41/6/46665928.pdf]

OECD. *Paying for Education.* 2010.

OECD. *PISA 2009 Results: What Students Know and Can Do,* 2010a. http://www.oecd.org/pisa/pisaproducts/48852548.pdf

OECD. Poverty has been rising, *Society at a Glance 2011: OECD Social Indicators.* 2011. [www.oecd.org/document/24/0,3746,en_2649_34637_2671576_1_1_1_1,00.html].

OECD. *Society at a Glance 2011 - OECD Social Indicators.* 2011. [www.oecd.org/els/social/indicators/SAG]

OECD. *Divided We Stand: Why Inequality Keeps Rising–Country Note: Canada.* 2011. [www.oecd.org/canada/49177689.pdf]

OECD. *Doing Better for Families.* 2011.

OECD. *Income inequality has been rising, Society at a Glance 2011: OECD Social Indicators.* 2011. [www.oecd.org]

OECD. *Divided We Stand: Why Inequality Keeps Rising,* 2011. [http://www.oecd.org/els/soc/dividedwestandwhyinequalitykeepsrising.htm]

OECD. *More public social spending in most countries since the 1980s, Society at a Glance 2011: OECD Social Indicators,* 2011. [www.oecd.org].

OECD. Governance, *OECD Better Life Initiative.* 2011. [www.oecdbetterlifeindex.org],

Oslo. *Strategy for Sustainable Development: Environment and Sustainability Status 2002, Urban Ecology Programme 2002-2014,* 2002.

Oslo. Department of Transport and Environmental Affairs. *Strategy for Sustainable Development: Environment and Sustainability Status 2002–Urban Ecology Programme 2002–2014.* 2002.

Oslo. Department of Transport and Environmental Affairs. *Reducing Greenhouse Gas Emissions and Improving Air Quality in Oslo–Guide 2006.* 2006.

Oslo. *Oslo Green Capital.* 2008.

Oslo. City Chief Commissioner's Department. *European Green Capital Application.* 2008.

Oslo. *Welcome to Boligbygg: Information for our residents.* 2010.

Palme, J. *The Nordic Model and the Modernisation of Social Protection in Europe.* Nordic Council of Ministers, Copenhagen, 1999.

Palme, J. *Welfare in Sweden: The Balance Sheet for the 1990s.* 2002.

Patz, J.A. et al. Impact of regional climate change on human health, *Nature,* vol. 17, no. 438, 2005, p. 310-317.

Peden, M., R. Scurfild and D. Sleet. *Rapport mondial sur la prévention des traumatismes dûs aux accidents de la circulation.* Geneva, World Health Organization, 2004.

Phelan, J.C. and B.G. Link. Controlling disease and creating disparities: a fundamental cause perspective, *Journals of Gerontology,* vol. 60B, no. 2 (Special), October 2005, p. 27-33.

Phipps, S. *Does Policy Affect Outcomes for young Children? An Analysis with International Microdata.* (Document W-00-1E), Human Resources Development Canada–Applied Research Branch of Strategic Policy, 1999.

Phipps, S.A. et al. Poverty and the extent of child obesity in Canada, Norway and the United States. *Obesity Reviews,* vol. 7, no. 1, February 2006, p. 5-12.

PolitiquesSociales.net. *Suède – Note synthèse, 2006.* [www.politiquessociales.net]

Pope, C.A., M. Ezzati and D.W. Dockery. Fine-particulate air pollution and life expectancy in the United States. *New England Journal of Medicine,* vol. 360, 2009, p. 376-386.

Poulton, R. et al. Association between children's experience of socioeconomic disadvantage and adult health: a life-course study. *Lancet,* vol. 360, 2002, p. 1640-1645.

Quebec. Assemblée nationale du Québec. La présence féminine. 15 oct. 2012. [www.assnat.qc.ca/fr/patrimoine/femmes1.html]

Quebec. Institut de la statistique du Québec. Taux de faible revenu, MFR, seuils après impôt, particuliers, municipalités régionales de comté et ensemble du Québec, 1997-2008, 2011. [www.stat.gouv.qc.ca]

Quebec. Institut de la statistique du Québec. Taux de faible revenu, effectif à faible revenu and effectif total, MFR-seuils après impôt, familles, particuliers hors famille and particuliers, RA and ensemble du Québec, 1997-2009, 2012. [www.stat.gouv.qc.ca/ donstat/societe/famls_mengs_niv_vie/revenus_depense/index.htm#faible_revenu]

Quebec. Ministère de la Santé and des Services sociaux du Québec. *Riches de tous nos enfants – La pauvreté and ses répercussions sur la santé des jeunes de moins de 18 ans,* Québec, 2007.

Quebec. Office des personnes handicapées du Québec. *Jeu questionnaire – Comment s'informer en testant ses connaissances sur les réalités vécues par les personnes handicapées ?* 2011.

Ranjit, N. et al. Material hardship alters the diurnal rhythm of salivary cortisol. *International Journal of Epidemiology*, vol. 34, no. 5, 2005, p. 1138-1143.

Raphael, D., T. Bryant and M. Rioux. *Staying Alive: Critical Perspectives on Health, Illness, and Health Care.* Canadian Scholars' Press, Toronto, 2006.

Ray, R., J.C. Gornick and J. Schmitt. *Parental Leave Policies in 21 Countries: Assessing Generosity and Gender Equality.* Center for Economic and Policy Research, Washington, 2009.

Raynault, M.-F. and D. Côté. *Synthèse de connaissances sur les politiques des pays nordiques qui contribuent à réduire les inégalités sociales de santé.* Report to Instituts de recherche en santé du Canada [IRSC]), Centre de recherche Léa-Roback sur les inégalités sociales de santé, Montréal, 2008.

Raynault, M.-F. *Santé and pauvreté: entre l'héroïsme and la dépression.* National Film Board, 2004. [www.citoyen.onf.ca/sante-et-pauvrete-entre-l-heroisme-et-la-depression]

Raynault, M.-F. et al. *Pauvreté and monoparentalité: Ce que peuvent nous apprendre les comparaisons internationales and interprovinciales croisant situations sociales and politiques publiques.* Report to Fonds québécois de recherche Société and culture [FQRSC], Centre de recherche Léa-Roback sur les inégalités sociales de santé, Montréal, 2010.

Reeves, F. *Planète cœur: santé cardiaque and environnement.* MultiMondes/CHU Sainte-Justine, Montréal, 2011.

Ross, N. et al. Relation between income inequality and mortality in Canada and in the United States: cross sectional assessment using census data and vital statistics. *British Medical Journal*, vol. 320, no. 7239, 2000, p. 898-902.

Roy, J.-P. Socioeconomic status and health: a neurobiological perspective. *Medical Hypotheses*, vol. 62, no. 2, 2003, p. 222-227.

Roy, J.-P. Statut socio-économique and santé: une perspective neurobiologique. In *Les inégalités sociales de santé au Québec*, Presses de l'Université de Montréal, 2008.

Rubenson, K. The Nordic model of lifelong learning. *Compare*, vol. 36, no. 3, 2006, p. 327-341.

Sahlin, I. The staircase of transition, *Innovation*, vol. 18, no. 2, 2005, p. 115-136.

Save the Children. *Women on the Front Lines of Health Care—State of the World's Mothers 2010*. Westport (CT)/London (UK), 2010.

Seeman, T. et al. Socio-economic differentials in peripheral biology: Cumulative allostatic load. *Annals of the New York Academy of Sciences*, vol. 1186, February 2010, p. 223-239.

Séguin, L. et al. Duration of poverty and child health in the Quebec Longitudinal Study of Child Development: longitudinal analysis of a birth cohort. *Pediatrics*, vol. 119, no. 5, 2007, p. e1063-e1070.

Séguin, L. et al. Understanding the dimensions of socioeconomic status that influence toddlers' health: unique impact of lack of money for basic needs in Quebec's birth cohort. *Journal of Epidemiology and Community Health*, vol. 59, no. 1, January 2005, p. 42-48.

Sherman, A. *Income Inequality Hits Record Levels, New CBO Data Show*. Center on Budget and Policy Priorities, Washington, 2007.

Shonkoff, J.P., W.T. Boyce and B.S. McEwen. Neuroscience, molecular biology, and the childhood roots of health disparities: building a new framework for health promotion and disease prevention. *Journal of the American Medical Association*, vol. 301, no. 21, 2009, p. 2252-2259.

Skär, L. and M. Tamm. My assistant and I: disabled children's and adolescents' roles and relationships to their assistants. *Disability and Society*, vol. 16, no. 7, 2001, p. 917-931.

Skedinger, P. *Sweden: A Minimum Wage Model in Need of Modification?* Research Institute of Industrial Economics, Working Paper no. 774, 2008.

Smargiassi, A. et al. Traffic intensity, dwelling value, and hospital admissions for respiratory disease among the elderly in Montreal (Canada): a case-control analysis. *Journal of Epidemiology and Community Health*, vol. 60, no. 6, June 2006, p. 507-512.

Smith, R. Countering child poverty. *British Medical Journal*, vol. 322, May 12, 2001, p. 1137-1138.

Spencer, N. *Poverty and Child Health*. (2nd edition), Radcliffe Medical Press, Oxon, 2000.

Spencer, N. Social, economic, and political determinants of child health, *Pediatrics*, vol. 112, no. 3, (Supplement), 2003, p. 704-706.

Srinivasan, S. et al. Creating healthy communities, healthy homes, healthy people: initiating a research agenda on the built environment and public health. *American Journal of Public Health*, vol. 93, no. 9, 2003, p. 1446-1450.

Stein, G. How Sweden affords the world's best paid parental leave, 2010. [www.muchissaidinjest.com/2010/11/04/how-sweden-affords-the-best-paid-paternity-leave-in-the-world/]

Stockholm. *Stockholm's Action Programme Against Greenhouse Gas Emissions*. 2002.

Stockholm. *Care for Families in Need*. 2007. [www.stockholm.se]

Stockholm. *Care for the Homeless*. 2007.

Stockholm. *Application for European Green Capital Award*. 2008.

Stockholm. *The Stockholm Environment Programme 2008-2011—Overarching goals and priorities*. 2008. [http://miljobarometern.stockholm.se/content/docs/mp/miljop-rogram2008_eng.pdf]

Stockholm. *Stockholm–A City for climate protection*. 2009. [www.stockholm.se]

Stockholm. *Family and Social Welfare*. 2011. [international.stockholm.se/Stockholm-by-theme/Welfare/]

Stockholm. Environment and Health Administration. *Promoting Clean Cars: Case Study of Stockholm and Sweden*. BioEthanol for Sustainable Transport (BEST), project no. TREN/05/FP6EN/S07.53807/019854, 2009. [http://www.best-europe.org/upload/BEST_documents/incentives/D.5.12%20Promoting%20Clean%20Cars%20Report.pdf]

Stockholm News. Fewer women in parliament with Sweden Democrats. 2010.[www.stockholmnews.com/more.aspx?NID=5994]

Strobel, P. Présentation du dossier Le modèle nordique de protection sociale sous le choc des réformes. *Revue française des affaires sociales*, vol. 4, no. 4, 2003.

Sweden. Parliament of Sweden. *Social Insurance Act 1999*.

Sweden. Parliament of Sweden. *The distribution of seats in the Ricksdagen*. 2010. [www.riksdagen.se]

Sweden. Parliament of Sweden. *Women in the Riksdag*. 2010. [www.riksdagen.se]

Sweden. Ministry of the Environment. *Agencies reporting to the Ministry of the Environment*. 2007. [www.sweden.gov.se/sb/d/2066/a/21984]

Sweden. Ministry of Justice. *Sweden's Roma; a national minority*. Fact sheet, 2003. [http://www.manskligarattigheter.se/dynamaster/file_archive/030625/389adc059ceaed09b-6f9a0bcec11c5a7/Fakta_Ju%2003.11e.pdf]

Sweden. Ministry of Health and Social Affairs. *Sweden's Strategy Report for Social Protection and Social Inclusion 2006-2008*. 2006.

Sweden. Ministry of Health and Social Affairs. *Financial Family Policy*. 2007.

Sweden. *The regional level*. 2004. [www.sweden.gov.se/sb/d/2858/a/16193]

Sweden. Needs-tested allowances. 2010. [www.sweden.gov.se]

Sweden. Divisions and secretariats. 2011. [www.sweden.gov.se/sb/d/3008/a/18108]

Sweden. Enhanced consultation with civil society. 2011. [www.sweden.gov.se/sb/d/14295/a/159035]

Sweden. Evaluation of the prohibition of the purchase of sexual service. 2011. [www.regeringen.se/sb/d/13420/a/151488?setEnableCookies=true]

Sweden. Gender mainstreaming. 2011. [www.sweden.gov.se/sb/d/4096/a/125215]

Sweden. Legislation on the purchase of sexual services. 2011. [www.sweden.gov.se/sb/d/4096/a/119861]

Sweden. National Agency for Education. *The Swedish School System*. 2005. [www.skolverket.se]

Sweden. National Board of Housing, Building and Planning. Constructing and housing, 2010. [www.boverket.se]

Sweden. National Board of Health and Welfare. *Personal Assistance and Assistance benefit*. Leaflet no. 2006-114-20, 2006.

Sweden. Statistics Sweden. Women and men in Sweden–Facts and figures 2006, 2006. [www.scb.se/statistik/_publikationer/LE0202_2006A01_BR_X10ST0602.pdf]

Sweden. National Agency for Education. *Pre-school in transition – A national evaluation of the Swedish pre-school.* Stockholm, 2004.

Sweden. National Agency for Education. *The Swedish School System.* 2005. [www.skolverket.se]

Sweden. National Agency for Education. *Ten years after the pre-school reform – A national evaluation of the Swedish pre-school.* Stockholm, 2008.

Sweden. National Agency for Education. *Läroplan för förskolan, Reviderad 2010.* Stockholm, 2010.

Sweden. National Board of Housing, Building and Planning. *Constructing and housing.* 2010. [www.boverket.se]

Sweden. *Swedish Association of Public Housing Companies (SABO). Housing market.* 2010. [http://www.sabo.se/om_sabo/english/Sidor/default.aspx]

Sweden. Swedish Social Insurance Agency. *Insured when you Live or Work in Sweden.* 2007.

Swedish Institute. *L'accueil de l'enfance en Suède.* 2005. [www.sweden.se/fr/Accueil/ Faits-en-bref/La-Suede-en-bref/La-societe/Accueil-de-lenfance/]

Swedish Institute. *Disability Policies in Sweden.* 2000.

Swedish Institute. *Equality between women and men. Fact sheet. 2004.* [www.sweden.se]

Swedish Institute. *Equality between women and men in Sweden: areas of responsibility– employment and gender equality.* Fact sheet, 2006. [www.sweden.gov.se]

Swedish Institute. *Swedish disability policy – Fact Sheet.* 2006a. [www.sweden.se]

Swedish Institute. *The Swedish system of government.* 2006b. [www.sweden.se]

Swedish Institute. *Swedish Health Care.* 2007.

Swedish Institute. *Needs-tested allowances.* 2010. [www.sweden.gov.se]

Swedish Institute. *Swedish disability policy: Dignity and democracy – Fact Sheet.* 2010a. [www.sweden.se/upload/Sweden_se/english/factsheets/SI/SI_FS87p_Swedish_dis- ability_policy/FS14-Disability-policy-low-resolution.pdf]

Swedish Institute. *Parental leave.* 2011. [www.sweden.se]

Swedish Institute. *Residence-based benefits.* 2011a. [www.sweden.se]

Swedish Institute. The Swedish system of government, *Facts about Sweden,* 2011b. [www.sweden.se/eng/Home/Society/Government-politics/Facts/Swedish- System-of-Government/]

Turner, B. and C. Whitehead Reducing housing subsidy: Swedish housing policy in an international context. *Urban Studies,* vol. 39, no. 2, 2002, p. 201-217.

UK. Department for Environment, Food and Rural Affairs. *Sustainable development indicators in your pocket 2007: An update of the UK Government Strategy indicators.* London, 2007.

UN. *The Millenium Development Goals Report 2007.* [www.un.org/millenniumgoals/ pdf/mdg2007.pdf]

UNDP. *Millenium Development Goals and Beyond 2015. Goal 3: Promote Gender equality and empower women.* 2013. https://www.un.org/millenniumgoals/gender.shtml

UNDP. *Droits de l'homme and développement humain – Rapport mondial sur le développement humain,* 2000.

UNDP. *La coopération internationale à la croisée des chemins – L'aide, le commerce and la sécurité dans un monde marqué par les inégalités – Rapport mondial sur le développement humain,* 2005.

UNDP. *Human Development Report 2006–Beyond scarcity: Power, Poverty and the Global Water Crisis,* 2006.

UNDP. *La lutte contre le changement climatique: un impératif de solidarité humaine dans un monde divisé – Rapport mondial sur le développement humain 2007/2008,* New York, 2007.

UNDP. *Lever les barrières: Mobilité and développement humains – Rapport mondial sur le développement humain,* 2009.

UNDP. *La vraie richesse des nations: les chemins du développement humain – Rapport sur le développement humain,* 2010.

UNDP. Millenium Development Goals. *Objectif 3: Promouvoir l'égalité des sexes and l'autonomisation des femmes,* 2011. https://www.un.org/millenniumgoals/gender.shtml

UNDP. *Droits de l'homme and développement humain – Rapport mondial sur le développement humain,* 2000.

UNDP. *La coopération internationale à la croisée des chemins – L'aide, le commerce and la sécurité dans un monde marqué par les inégalités – Rapport mondial sur le développement humain,* 2005.

UNDP *Human Development Report 2006–Beyond scarcity: Power, Poverty and the Global Water Crisis,* 2006.

UNDP *La lutte contre le changement climatique: un impératif de solidarité humaine dans un monde divisé – Rapport mondial sur le développement humain 2007/2008,* New York, 2007.

UNDP. *Lever les barrières: Mobilité and développement humains – Rapport mondial sur le développement humain,* 2009.

UNDP. *La vraie richesse des nations: les chemins du développement humain – Rapport sur le développement humain,* 2010.

UNESCO. *Education for All by 2015–Will we make it?,* Oxford University Press, Paris, 2007.

UNICEF. Measuring child poverty: new league tables of child poverty in the world's richest countries. *Innocenti Report Card 10,* UNICEF Innocenti Research Center, Florence, 2012. [www.unicef-irc.org/publications/pdf/rc10_eng.pdf]

UNICEF. *UNICEF Report Card 10: Measuring Child Poverty, Canadian Companion,* 2010. [www.unicef.ca/sites/default/files/imce_uploads/TAKE%20ACTION/ADVOCATE/DOCS/canadian_companion_updated.pdf.]

UNICEF. The big picture, 2007.

UNICEF. *Child Poverty in Rich Countries*. Innocenti Report Card 6. UNICEF Innocenti Research Centre, Florence, 2005. [www.unicef-irc.org/publications/pdf/repcard6e.pdf]

Union des familles françaises. *Garde des bébés – Quatre pays comparés à la France: Finlande, Norvège, Autriche and Allemagne*. 2007. [www.uniondesfamilles.org/accueil-bebe-europe.htm]

USA. Bureau of Labor Statistics–US Department of Labor. *Union Members Summary*. 2011.[www.bls.gov/news.release/union2.nro.htm]

USA. Central Intelligence Agency (CIA). Country comparison: Distribution of family income–GINI Index. *World Factbook*, 2011.

USA. Department of State. *2010 Human Rights Report: Denmark*. [www.state.gov/g/drl/rls/hrrpt/2010/eur/154421.htm]

Veall, M. *Top Income Share in Canada: Updates and Extensions*. McMaster University, 2010.

VisitDenmark. Partez à la découverte de Copenhague, 2008. [www.visitdenmark.com]

Vivre en Ville. *Vers des collectivités viables – À la découverte de villes durables d'Europe*. (Video), Québec, 2004.

Weich, S. and M. Blanchard. Mental health and the built environment: cross-sectional survey of individual and contextual risk factors for depression. *The British Journal of Psychiatry*, vol. 180, 2002, p. 428-433.

Wein, H. Stress and disease: new perspectives, *Word on Health*. National Institutes of Health, 2000.

Whitehead, M. and G. Dahlgren. *Levelling up (part 1): a discussion paper on concepts and principles for tackling social inequities in health*. WHO Collaborating Centre for Policy Research on Social Determinants of Health–University of Liverpool, Copenhagen, 2006, p. 14-15.

Whitehead, M. *The Health Divide: Inequalities in Health in the 1980's*. Health Education Council, London, 1987.

Whitehead, M. A typology of actions to tackle social inequalities in health. *Journal of Epidemiology and Community Health*, vol. 61, no. 6, juin 2007, p. 473-478.

WHO Commission on Social Determinants of Health. *Closing the gap in a generation: Health equity through action on the social determinants of health. Final Report*. World Health Organization, Geneva, 2008, p. 87. [http://whqlibdoc.who.int/publications/2008/9789241563703_eng.pdf?ua=1]

Wikipedia. Government agencies in Sweden, 2011. [en.wikipedia.org/wiki/Government_agencies_in_Sweden],

Wikipedia. Norwegian government agencies, 2011a. [en.wikipedia.org/wiki/Norwegian_government_agencies],

Wikipedia. Politics of Denmark, 2011b. [en.wikipedia.org/wiki/Politics_of_Denmark#Proportional_representation_and_elections]

Wikipedia. Denmark, 2011c. [en.wikipedia.org/wiki/Denmark]

Wilkinson, R. and M. Marmot (eds). *Social Determinants of Health — The Solid Facts.* World Health Organization, Copenhagen, 2004. [www.euro.who.int/_data/assets/pdf_file/0005/98438/e81384.pdf]

Wilkinson, R.G. and K.E. Pickett The problems of relative deprivation: why some societies do better than others. *Social Science & Medicine,* vol. 65, no. 9, November 2007, p. 1965-1978.

Wilkinson, R. and K. Pickett. *The Spirit Level: Why Greater Equality Makes Societies Stronger.* New York, Bloomsbury Press, 2009.

Williams, D.R. et al. Race, socioeconomic status, and health: complexities, ongoing challenges, and research opportunities. *Annals of the New York Academy of Sciences,* vol. 1186, févr. 2010, p. 69-101.

Willson, A.E. 'Fundamental causes' of health disparities: A comparative analysis of Canada and the Unites States. *International Sociology,* vol. 24, no. 1, January 2009, p. 93-113.

Wood, D. Effect of child and family poverty on child health in the United States. *Pediatrics,* vol. 112, no. 3, September 2003, p. 707-711.

World Economic Forum. *The Global Competitiveness Report 2004-2005–Executive Summary.* 2005.

World Economic Forum. *The Global Competitiveness Report 2007-2008.* Geneva, 2008.

World Economic Forum. *The Global Competitiveness Report 2009-2010.* Geneva, 2010.

World Economic Forum. *The Global Competitiveness Report 2010-2011.* Geneva, 2010.

World Economic Forum. *The Global Gender Gap Report.* Geneva, 2010.

Yalnizyan, A. *The Rise of Canada's Richest 1%.* Canadian Centre for Policy Alternatives, Ottawa, 2010.

Achevé d'imprimer
sur les presses de
Imprimerie H.L.N.
Imprimé au Canada - Printed in Canada